Strategy
Express

John Middleton and Bob Gorzynski

- Fast track route to mastering all aspects of strategy

- Covers all the fundamentals of successful strategy, from developing a compelling vision to knowing your customers, and from fostering creativity to making it happen

- Examples and lessons from benchmark companies, including Encyclopaedia Britannica, Sears, Seven-Eleven Japan and ideas from the smartest thinkers

- Includes a glossary of key concepts and a comprehensive resources guide

>>EXPRESS EXEC.COM<<
essential management thinking at your fingertips

The right of John Middleton and Bob Gorzynski to be identified as the authors of this work has been asserted in accordance with the Copyright, Designs and Patents Act 1988

First published 2002 by
Capstone Publishing (a Wiley company)
8 Newtec Place
Magdalen Road
Oxford OX4 1RE
United Kingdom
http://www.capstoneideas.com

CIP catalogue records for this book are available from the British Library and the US Library of Congress

ISBN 1-84112-218-1

Printed and bound in Great Britain

This book is printed on acid-free paper

Substantial discounts on bulk quantities of Capstone books are available to corporations, professional associations and other organizations. Please contact Capstone for more details on +44 (0)1865 798 623 or (fax) +44 (0)1865 240 941 or (e-mail) info@wiley-capstone.co.uk

Contents

Introduction to

ExpressExec

ExpressExec is 3 million words of the latest management thinking compiled into 10 modules. Each module contains 10 individual titles forming a comprehensive resource of current business practice written by leading practitioners in their field. From brand management to balanced scorecard, ExpressExec enables you to grasp the key concepts behind each subject and implement the theory immediately. Each of the 100 titles is available in print and electronic formats.

Through the ExpressExec.com Website you will discover that you can access the complete resource in a number of ways:

» printed books or e-books;
» e-content – PDF or XML (for licensed syndication) adding value to an intranet or Internet site;
» a corporate e-learning/knowledge management solution providing a cost-effective platform for developing skills and sharing knowledge within an organization;
» bespoke delivery – tailored solutions to solve your need.

Why not visit www.expressexec.com and register for free key management briefings, a monthly newsletter and interactive skills checklists. Share your ideas about ExpressExec and your thoughts about business today.

Please contact elound@wiley-capstone.co.uk for more information.

Introduction to Strategy

Why is the discipline of strategy so challenging? This chapter considers:

» the paradoxical nature of successful strategy;
» strategy as a state of mind as well as a set of tools and techniques.

KEEPING OUR FEET ON THE GROUND – A STRATEGIC TALE

Two explorers were trudging across the icy wastes. Suddenly a polar bear reared up from behind a glacier.

"What do we do now?" asked one of the men.

The other man knelt down, removed his snow-shoes and took a pair of sneakers out of his back-pack.

"It's pointless putting those on," said the first man. "Those bears can outrun any man."

"I know," said the other, "but I only have to run faster than you."

Source: *Positioning and Capability*, Develin & Partners

In 1980, Michael Porter first published his seminal work *Competitive Strategy*, which rewrote the ground rules for all those looking at strategy. Two years later, Tom Peters and Robert Waterman published *In Search of Excellence*, which quickly became an article of faith for managers around the globe.

Even so, around 20 years later, despite the widespread use of universal tonics such as total quality management and business process re-engineering, strategy is still at the centre of management debate and we seem no closer to understanding what makes an organization successful. Richard Pascale, a leading management writer, puts it nicely:

"The sobering truth is that our theories, models, and conventional wisdom combined appear no better at predicting an organization's ability to sustain itself than if we were to rely on random chance."
From "Managing on the Edge", Penguin, New York, 1990

Strategy Express seeks to explain why strategy continues to excite, frustrate and intrigue us. It traces the history of strategic planning in business and looks at the major components of strategy in the 1990s. It examines the conventional strategic framework and asks how useful this paradigm has been in the past for understanding organizational success. Finally, it looks at current developments in strategic thinking and suggests an expanded framework for understanding and implementing the strategic process.

UNDERSTANDING STRATEGY – LIVING WITH PARADOX

Why is it that strategy remains so challenging? The answer lies partly in the paradoxical nature of strategy. Strategies that have ultimately proved successful often appeared contradictory or even absurd at first sight. Think of Honda's entry into the US auto market, the desire of British Airways to become the "world's favourite airline" or the vision of British Steel to become the first internationally-based steel company, ahead of its Japanese, Korean and US rivals.

Moreover, "good" strategies often challenge preconceived ideas of the world, or what we consider reasonable or possible. Thus strategy becomes as much a *state of mind* as a set of tools and techniques. To see some of the paradoxes underlying strategy today, look at a number of statements, which seek to explain the nature of successful strategy. Each statement reflects some aspect of current management thinking (Table 1.1).

Table 1.1   What successful strategies are based on.

» A vision of the future	» A firm footing in reality
» Re-inventing the organization *and* its industry	» Careful matching of organizational strengths to market opportunities
» Stretching the organization beyond what is currently possible	» Core competencies (the key strengths acquired, and relationships developed by the organization over time)
» Creating a shared vision of the future by empowering people throughout the organization	» Strong charismatic leadership
» Seeing the big picture	» Attention to detail

It is not hard to accept that *each* of these statements is true, or at least that each conveys some essential element of successful strategy.

However, at first sight, it is tempting to conclude that there is a trade-off operating between the statements on the left-hand side with those on the right; that there is an implicit choice between the alternatives involved. Indeed many organizations do assume exactly this, often at great cost to themselves. In the West, for example, it was accepted for years that just such a choice existed between the cost of a product and its quality, an assumption that was spectacularly debunked by the Japanese.

As with cost and quality, close examination of all the statements above will show that there is a paradox operating. Successful strategy depends not on a choice of *either/or*, but on the *simultaneous existence of both qualities*. Paradox is at the heart of many of the apparently contradictory messages from management gurus, academics and writers. Organizations are exhorted to "stick to the knitting," decentralize, empower, direct, dream, apply common sense, be flexible and adaptive, lead the industry, benchmark, re-invent themselves, absorb best practise, delight the customer, become quality oriented, remain lean and mean, establish community, kindle the human spirit, and meet the expectations of the stock market or funding body. It is no wonder that many business and community leaders take management fads with a pinch of salt. As *The Economist* has pointed out:

> "For all the hype, fad-based management fails to deliver. Quality programs are launched with a great fanfare, then fade away: Florida Power & Light, an electricity company, at one time boasted an 85-person quality department and 1,900 quality teams, but saw little improvement in its services. Cutting management layers often disrupts internal communications, as firms such as Nynex and Sears, Roebuck have discovered. Many companies – among them Compaq and Harley-Davidson – have found outsourcing so hard to manage that some subcontracted production is now back in-house. And, according to the American Management Association, fewer than half of the firms that have downsized since 1990 have seen long-term improvements in quality, profitability or productivity."
>
> *"Instant Coffee as Management Theory", The Economist,*
> *January 25, 1997*

Even so, successful strategy almost always involves organizations in getting to grips with the kinds of paradox stated above, and meeting this challenge is one of the main themes of this book. However, understanding and working with paradox is not the same as reconciling a series of apparently contradictory statements into some grand strategic framework. It is an attempt to examine, and ultimately to go beyond, our current level of thinking. In the words of Gary Hamel and C.K. Prahalad in their leading work *Competing for the Future*:

"Much has been written about the need to manage tensions, trade-offs, paradoxes, and contradictions. Unfortunately much of this misses the point. The goal is not to find the narrow line between the unattractive extremes nor to maintain an uneasy balance between counterposed forces. In short, the goal is not to occupy the middle ground; it is to find the higher ground."

Definition of Terms

» The essence of strategy: developing an understanding of;
» the present situation (Where are we now?)
» the desired future position (Where do we want to be?)
» the path to take the organization from its present position into the future (How do we get there?).

''Thinking strategically starts with reflection on the deepest nature of an undertaking and on the central challenges that it poses''
Peter Senge, Director for the Centre of Organizational Learning at MIT's Sloan School of Management, in The Fifth Discipline.

A TRADITIONAL APPROACH TO STRATEGY

The strategic process has traditionally been focused in three key areas:

Developing key strengths or capabilities (sometimes known as *core competencies* or *distinctive capabilities*) which allow an organization to perform activities that are different from those of its rivals (either by performing different activities or by performing activities differently).

Identifying unmet customer needs in the marketplace that the organization can fulfil. This requires the organization to position itself in the marketplace by developing a *unique selling proposition* (USP), sometimes known as a *differentiated customer proposition* (DCP).

Developing tactical responses to the moves of competitors in the marketplace (often known as competitive strategy).

In addition, strategy is an iterative process, which is conducted at many levels within an organization (Table 2.1).

Table 2.1 Levels of strategy.

Corporate	The overall scope of an organization
Business	A strategic business unit (SBU) within an organization (or sometimes used as a generic term)
Competitive	How to compete in a market – often thought of as 'tactical' strategy
Operational	How each function contributes to the strategic vision, for example:
Finance	Measuring performance and resource utilization
Marketing	Assessing customer needs and market feedback
Human Resources	Making the best use of people

DEFINING STRATEGY

There are many definitions of strategy, a selection of which are reproduced below:

» *Johnson & Scholes*, 1997: The direction and scope of an organization over the long term: which achieves advantage for the organization through its configuration of resources within a changing environment, to meet the needs of markets, and to fulfil stakeholder expectations.

» *Gary Hamel, 1997*: Strategy is always, and I mean always, lucky foresight. Strategy is always serendipity. Strategy is always the product of a complex and unexpected interplay between ideas, information, concepts, personalities and desires.

» *John Kay*, 1993: Competitive strategy is concerned with the firm's position relative to its competitors in the markets which it has chosen. The strategy of the firm is the match between its internal capabilities and its external relationships.

» *Igor Ansoff*, 1994: Strategic management is a comprehensive procedure which starts with a strategic diagnosis and guides a firm through a series of additional steps which culminate in new products, markets and technologies, as well as new capabilities.

» *Henry Mintzberg*, 1994: Strategy is not the consequence of planning but the opposite: its starting point.

» *Bob Gorzynski*, 1998: Strategy is life: determining who you are, where you are headed and figuring out how to get there. It is the easiest and yet most difficult thing in the world.

Remember that strategy can also be:

» A state of mind predicated on organizational awareness. Simply put, the ability to see the organization in its broadest sense from the perspective of others (whether stakeholders or not).

» Daring to be different. Either in terms of operational excellence, customer intimacy or innovation (giving rise to competitive advantage) as a result of vision or industry foresight.

» Holistic, most often in terms of seeing a bigger picture than others see. Good strategies are often based on changing the rules of the game by redefining the industry box (strategy as revolution).

Michael Porter draws a distinction between *operational effectiveness* and *strategy*. Operational effectiveness is concerned with performing similar activities better than rivals (by improving productivity, quality, and speed using such tools as TQM, benchmarking and re-engineering). This is necessary for superior performance but not sufficient. In contrast, the essence of strategy is performing *different* activities from rivals or performing similar activities in *different* ways (by choosing a unique and valuable market position rooted in systems of activities that are much more difficult to match).

THE ESSENCE OF STRATEGY

All these definitions concern themselves (sometimes implicitly) with the future direction of the organization and the selection of a route map to guide the organization into that future. Accordingly strategy is concerned with developing an understanding of the present situation (Where are we now?), the desired future position (Where do we want to be?) and the path to take the organization from its present position into the future (How do we get there?).

There are many aspects to the strategic process but, at its core, strategy concerns itself with the creation of a unique and valuable position (Michael Porter, 1996). This requires an organization to excel at a particular set of activities in order to develop a *unique point of difference*, which matches *internal* capabilities with *external* market needs.

The single most important reason for the failure of strategy is not inadequate analytical rigor in decision-making, failure to understand markets, competitors or products, or even lack of executive insight into fundamental changes in the industry or environment. It is the fact that the vast majority of employees see absolutely no relationship between the strategy of their organizations and what is fundamentally important to them as human beings.

STRATEGIC TERMINOLOGY

Strategic terminology can be complex and confusing. Mnemonics such as MOST can be helpful:

» **M Mission** The essence or purpose of an organization.
» **O Objectives** The quantifiable goals which represent where the organization wishes to be in the foreseeable future.
» **S Strategy** How the organization intends to meet its objectives – the broad game plan.
» **T Tactics** The specific tasks and actions which the organization will undertake to achieve its objectives (Implementation).

However, simple frameworks such as MOST tend to understate the degree of interaction between different elements in the strategic process:

» The strategic development process is *not* sequential. It is iterative, with the processes of setting objectives, strategies and tactics deeply intertwined.
» In reality, the strategic process is messy and experimental with critical information and resources flowing from the bottom up. Hence one definition of strategy as "the management of ignorance."
» The basic ingredient of a good strategy – *insight into how to create value* – rarely emerges from the planning process. Instead, it originates from many varied and hard-to-control ways, some of which are more about implementation than strategic development.
» Strategy is deeply rooted in organizational *purpose* (what an organization exists to do) which requires a process of introspection not common in planning processes.

CLARIFYING STRATEGIC TERMINOLOGY

The strategic vocabulary can be confusing. Aims, objectives, and goals can mean different things in different organizations. The following definitions represent the generally-accepted definitions of the most commonly-used words related to strategy – and will be used consistently throughout this book.

» **Vision**: a picture of the future, often an intuitive leap of faith.

- » **Mission**: over-riding premise in line with the values and expectations of stakeholders.
- » **Goals**: general statement of aim or purpose (qualitative).
- » **Objectives**: more precise statement of goals (often quantitative).
- » **Strategies**: broad categories or types of actions to achieve objectives.
- » **Actions**: individual operational steps to implement strategies, also called "tasks".
- » **Control**: monitoring process to assess effectiveness of strategy, modifying accordingly.
- » **Reward**: pay-off.

Source: Adapted from *Exploring Corporate Strategy*, Johnson & Scholes, 1998, FT Prentice Hall.

The Evolution of Strategy

» Originally drawn from military models.
» Key models of strategy: natural selection; systematic planning; adaptive; cultural; political; visionary.
» 1960s: relatively stable environment with strong economic growth, which fostered a planning orientation. Assumed that the business world was predictable and rational.
» Paralysis by analysis.
» 1980: Porter's Five Forces model.
» 1990s and onward: increasingly strategy is viewed as an holistic discipline.

"It's tough to make predictions, especially about the future."
Attributed to movie mogul Sam Goldwyn

WINNERS AND LOSERS – THE LEGACY OF THE MILITARY METAPHOR

Strategy has always been concerned with *how* to do things. Conventionally, strategy is taken to mean the blueprint, game-plan or road map of organizational change. Since strategy has its origins in military usage, we tend to think of it in terms of plans of attack or defense, competitive battlefields, and winners and losers. This is unfortunate, as strategy is as much to do with understanding the *process of change* as with the tactics employed to deal with it. Moreover, strategy is more than a zero-sum game. It is not simply about competing for a bigger share of a finite market, it is about creating new markets to meet human needs in new and exciting ways. It is about *creating the future*. In the words of Gary Hamel and C. K. Prahalad:

"There is not one future but hundreds. There is no limit that says that most companies must be followers. Getting to the future first is not just about outrunning competitors bent on reaching the same prize. It is also about having one's own view of what the prize is. There can be as many prizes as runners; imagination is the only limiting factor."
"Competing for the future: breakthrough strategies for seizing control of your industry and creating the markets of tomorrow",
Harvard Business School Press, 1994

The military connotation is unfortunate in another, more obvious, way. Military strategy is the prerogative of generals; soldiers are expected merely to follow orders. While organizations frequently talk of empowerment and upward communication, when it comes to strategic decision-making, an essentially hierarchical mind-set often prevails. Sometimes, this is justified under the guise of the expertise required to understand the organization's complex environment. Sometimes, it simply reflects the personal egos of key executives. Whatever the case may be, the message sent out to the organization is a very damaging one; "the truth is, we just don't trust you." As Charles Handy points out:

> "Trust is at the heart of the matter. That seems obvious and trite, yet most of our organizations tend to be arranged on the assumption that people cannot be trusted or relied on, even in tiny matters."
>
> *"Trust and the virtual organization", Harvard Business Review, May/June 1995*

Moving away from the military metaphor requires a fundamental change in perspective; from the limited to the unlimited, from protective to creative, from sceptical to trusting, and from self-assurance to humility. It also requires seeing the part that all members of an organization play in challenging mind-sets, inventing new opportunities, and creating the future. It means appreciating that every position in an organization, however humble, is absolutely vital in the making of strategy. It means recognizing the part that we all play in creating the future. This seems a lot to ask, but nevertheless our best organizations can and do move away from the military metaphor.

The discipline of strategy has always incorporated new elements and strands. These strands are often interpreted as alternative ways of viewing strategy, but in reality they can be seen as reflecting different aspects of the external environment and/or different time periods.

In the 1960s, for example, organizations faced a relatively stable environment with strong economic growth, which fostered a planning orientation.

One of the seminal influences on the development of thinking about strategy in the 1950s and 1960s was Pulitzer Prize-winning business historian Alfred D. Chandler. His book *Strategy and Structure*, published in 1962, was characterized by an underlying assumption that organizations act in a rational, sequential manner. Chandler defined strategy as "the determination of the long-term goals and objectives of an enterprise, and the adoption of courses of action and the allocation of resources necessary for carrying out these goals." Growth resulted from the awareness of the opportunities and needs to employ existing or expanding resources more profitably and efficiently. He saw structure as "the design of the organization through which the enterprise is administered." Chandler's famous conclusion, that structure follows strategy, was accepted as a fact of corporate life for decades until challenged in the 1980s and 1990s by radical thinkers like Tom Peters and Richard Pascale.

In a similar vein, the academic and consultant Igor Ansoff was in 1965 offering a highly prescriptive approach to strategy and advocating a heavy reliance on the use of analytical tools. Ansoff's particular contribution to the evolution of thinking about business strategy was to provide a rational model and a set of concepts and tools by which strategic and planning decisions could be made.

According to the Ansoff Model of Strategic Planning, the strategic decision-making process consists of what Ansoff called a "cascade of decisions, starting with highly aggregated ones and proceeding toward the more specific." Central to this concept was the notion of gap analysis. In fact, more specifically, Ansoff's whole approach revolved around the gathering of potentially vast quantities of data. As a result, many of his followers found themselves encountering a phenomenon which came to be known as "paralysis by analysis" (Table 3.1).

Through the 1960s and 1970s, then, there was an over-riding view in the business world that the future was readily predictable and business strategy was the means by which an organization's future could be pinpointed, planned for, and effectively managed.

This world-view was perpetuated by Michael Porter, arguably the most influential thinker and writer on strategic issues to have emerged in the last 25 years. When his *Competitive Strategy* was published in 1980, Porter's generic strategies offered companies a rational and embraceable model for grasping and managing their future. According to Porter, a company finds itself in the midst of a set of competing forces that pit it not only against its direct competitors but also against its suppliers, customers, and those who may become its future competitors. Management's core challenge, he maintains, is to tighten the company's hold over its suppliers and customers and to find ways to keep existing and future competitors at bay, protecting the firm's strategic advantages and allowing it to benefit maximally from them.

The essence of this theory is simple: the objective of a company is to capture as much as possible of the value that is embodied in its

Table 3.1 Historical influences on strategy.

Model	Key elements
Natural selection	» Importance of environment » Increasing turbulence » Transformation versus change
Systematic planning	» Analytical tools that provide a framework for looking at problems and challenging the status quo
Adaptive: logical incrementalism	» Inter-active and iterative management process » Emergent, opportunist and imposed strategies » Common sense (an oxymoron)
Cultural	» Deeper level of basis assumptions and beliefs shared by members of an organization (many unconscious) that define an organization's view of self and environment
Political	» Influence of internal and external interest groups » Power (control of information) » Horse trading (bargaining and negotiation)
Visionary	» Charismatic leaders » Product and change champions » Gut feel and intuition

Source: Adapted from Johnson & Scholes. *Exploring Corporate Strategy*

products and services. The problem is that there are others – customers, suppliers, and competitors among them – who want to do the same. As the economists point out, if there is genuine, free competition, companies can make no profits above the market value of their resources. The purpose of strategy, therefore, is to prevent such open and free competition: to claim the largest share of the pie while preventing others from eating your lunch, to mix metaphors.

The main problem with Porter's concept of companies, which has shaped the thinking of a generation of managers, is that it is based on a static view of the world, in which the size of the economic pie is given and finite. In this zero-sum world, all that is then left to be decided is how the pie is to be divided up, and corporate profits must indeed come at a cost to society.

Although Porter's take on strategy retains its adherents to this day, the 1990s saw a radical transformation of strategy away from its roots in long-term planning to a more holistic discipline concerned with aligning the organization to a rapidly changing world. Christopher A. Bartlett and Sumantra Ghoshal have explored this change in a series of articles for the Harvard Business Review between November 1994 and May 1995. The authors explored a business environment in which over-capacity was the norm, markets were global, lines separating businesses were fuzzy, and, with equal access to technology, early-market entry advantages became minimal.

Bartlett and Ghoshal suggested that a change in management doctrine was needed to match this new landscape, namely that:

» Senior managers should change their own priorities and way of thinking. They should expand their focus from devising formal structures to developing organizational purpose.
» Companies should shift from top-down direction by managers who set the company vision, and should encourage instead bottom-up initiatives from operating units, which are closest to customers.
» Top managers should shift from directing and correcting middle and frontline managers to creating an environment in which individuals monitor themselves.

In short, they argued that the traditional strategic paradigm,[1] in which organizational structures and systems supported strategy, was being replaced by a more humanistic paradigm which relied more heavily on defining the purpose and vision of the organization and developing the skills to meet this vision.

Today, most strategic commentators maintain that a robust planning framework is still absolutely vital to the success of an organization, but that it is clearly no longer sufficient by itself, in view of very rapid rates of change. Accordingly, in the early years of the twenty-first century, the emphasis has shifted to factors which allow organizations to develop adaptability and flexibility (Table 3.2).

Table 3.2 The changing nature of strategy.

Old paradigm		New paradigm	
Model	**Underlying metaphors**	**Model**	**Underlying metaphors**
Strategy Defines	Military (Battle plans)	*Purpose* Defines	Calling/Vision or Mission
Structure Supports	Architecture/ Building	*Processes* Supports	Flows/Activities/ Core competencies/ Key capabilities
Systems	Machine/ Control/ Vertical flows	*People*	Humanistic/ 'random' flows
Benefits	Discipline Focus Control	**Benefits**	Knowledge Innovation Flexibility Liberation (of the human spirit)

Source: Adapted from Christopher A. Bartlett and Sumantra Ghoshal, *Harvard Business Review* (three articles between November 1994 and May 1995)

NOTE

1 A paradigm is a constellation of concepts, values, perceptions and practices shared by a community which forms a particular vision of reality and collective mood that is the basis of the way that the community organizes itself.

The E-Dimension

» The Internet offers huge scope for cost-cutting.
» The hare, the tortoise, and the Internet.
» Internet-only companies carry less organizational baggage.
» He who pays the piper . . . the power of the buyer.
» The rise and fall of the middleman
» Internet-based alliances.
» Conclusion: Despite a faltering of the dot-com sector, the reach of the Internet is bringing more intensified competition just about everywhere.

"In periods of transition such as the one we have been going through, it often appears as if there are new rules of competition. But as market forces play out, as they are now, the old rules regain their currency. The creation of true economic value once again becomes the final arbiter of business success."

Michael Porter, writing in Harvard Business Review, March
2001

New century: new economy, and new economics. When, early in 2000, the UK travel ticket organization lastminute.com's flotation gave the company the same market value as venerable bricks-and-mortar retailer WH Smith, it did seem to confirm that the economic paradigm had been shifted by the upstart online businesses. The message seemed to be "Don't worry about this year's numbers; just imagine the potential a few years down the road." Share prices soared.

Then the markets tumbled, and a relentless succession of high-profile dot-com humiliations confirmed that the Internet's period of grace was officially over. So what lesson is there to learn from all this?

Many have argued that the introduction of the Internet into business practices renders the old rules of strategy and competitive advantage obsolete. According to Harvard Business School professor Michael Porter, the opposite is true. He has written:

"The only way [for companies to be more profitable than the average performer] is by achieving a sustainable competitive edge – by operating at a lower cost, by commanding a premium price, or by doing both."

"Strategy and the Internet", Harvard Business Review 2001

Because the Internet tends to weaken industry profitability without providing proprietary operational advantages, it is more important than ever for companies to distinguish themselves through strategy. The winners will be those who view the Internet as a complement to, not a cannibal of, traditional ways of competing.

Many of the early Internet pioneers, both the newly-minted dot-coms and those well-established companies seeking an on-line presence, have competed in ways that violate nearly every principle in the strategy rule-book. As Porter puts it:

"Rather than focus on profits, they have chased customers indiscriminately through discounting, channel incentives, and advertising. Rather than concentrate on delivering value that earns an attractive price from customers, they have pursued indirect revenues such as advertising and click-through fees. Rather than make trade-offs they have rushed to offer every conceivable product or service."

The good news is that it did not have to be this way – these were bad strategic choices but they were not the only options available. And these choices had little to do with the inherent business potential of the Internet.

In fact, when it comes to reinforcing a distinctive strategy, Porter maintains that the Internet provides a better technological platform than any previous generation of IT.

For most existing industries and established companies, the Internet rarely cancels out important sources of competitive advantage; if anything, it is more likely to increase the value of those sources. But over time, says Porter, the Internet itself will be neutralised as a source of advantage as soon as all companies begin to embrace its technology.

When this happens, we may well see a return to the good old days, and competitive advantages will once again explicitly derive from traditional strengths such as unique products, proprietary content, and distinctive physical activities. Internet technology may be able to fortify those advantages, but it is unlikely to supplant them.

The message, then, is clear. Gaining competitive advantage in the post-Internet business world does not require a radically new approach to business; and it certainly does not require the abandonment of classic economic principles that can still offer strategic value in a market place that depends on cutting-edge information technology.

No, gaining competitive advantage in the early years of the twenty-first century is still reliant on applying proven principles of effective strategy.

Sources of strategic advantage rest where they have always rested – in cost competitiveness, product differentiation, ease of entering and exiting markets, and so on. The significance of the Internet is in how it can impact on these traditional battlegrounds. Here are some examples:

The Internet offers huge scope for cost-cutting

General Electric now does more business on its own private on-line market place than do all the public B2B exchanges put together. Siemens hopes to cut its annual costs in the medium term by 3 to 5% by its use of the Internet. And there is room for more. One estimate quoted recently in *The Economist* ("Older, wiser, webbier", June 30, 2001) puts the cost of e-procurement per order placed for routine office purchases at only 10% of physical procurement costs. Low-cost airlines like Go and Ryanair have slashed their costs by using the Internet to dispense with the need for tickets and to cut out travel agents. Even so, very few companies have so far got to grips with the cost-saving potential of the net. In 2001, a survey by the National Association of Manufacturers found that only around 30% of American manufacturers were using the Internet to sell or to procure products or services.

The hare, the tortoise, and the Internet

Another myth, disputed by Michael Porter and others, is that the Internet offers huge 'first-mover' advantages. However, companies that took to the Internet relatively late and with some caution do not necessarily seem to have suffered; if anything, they seem to have gained from being able to avoid the mistakes and the huge spending of the pioneers. The fate of many Internet retailers has shown that established companies can catch up relatively easily. The contrast between Britain's biggest supermarket chain, Tesco, selling its e-buying system to America's Safeway, and the collapse of Webvan, the most ambitious and best-capitalized online grocery chain, is instructive. There is also a strong suggestion that the Internet could well be lowering, not raising, barriers to entry.

Internet-only companies carry less organizational baggage

The big boys are not having it all their own way. The arrival of new, Internet-based firms that are more agile and innovative than the giants is shaking up whole industries and business sectors. Without question, the Internet is helping to put some small, agile newcomers on a par with large corporations and letting them compete head on with them for new business. Just as Microsoft came from virtually nowhere to usurp the market of mighty IBM, so a few years later Netscape appeared overnight and threatened to undermine the market (and the size) of Microsoft. Who will be next? And where will they come from?

He who pays the piper ...

Another consequence of the growth of the Internet as a business medium, says Robert Baldock in his book *The Last Days of the Giants?*, has been a shift in power from the seller to the buyer. According to Baldock, "*the convergence of computing, communications and content in the shape of personal computers (PCs) hooked up over a network to the Internet has triggered a revolution in the way business is conducted. Users of these technologies have 24 hour access to almost everything, everywhere.*"

The rise and fall of the middleman

Part of the paradox of the Internet is that intermediaries are blessed under one business model and cursed under another.

On the positive side, Internet-based search agents make it possible for these users to track down the cheapest products in seconds, and new Internet-based intermediaries (called Infomediaries) have created a new form of commerce whereby the buyer sets the price, not the seller.

On the other hand, according to the "cursed" theory, information technology puts producers directly in contact with their customers, collapsing the distribution chain, wiping out all those who have made their living by taking orders or breaking big lots into smaller lots. A spooky technical term has been coined for this process: disintermediation. "Middleman functions between consumers and producers are being eliminated," the futurist Don Tapscott wrote in the influential best-seller *The Digital Economy*. Patrick McGovern, chairman of International Data Group, the world's largest high-tech publisher, is even more dour. "*The intermediary is doomed,*" he wrote in Forbes ASAP. "*Technology strips him of effectiveness.*"

THE BUSINESS MODEL OF EBAY

Traditional corporate strategy centres on establishing defensive strategic positions, building assets, and driving synergies from different combinations of assets and/or businesses. Newer models of strategy, however, stress the quality of the strategic process itself, which underpins the ability of the organization to define the "rules of the game" in its industry, rather than simply react to them. This leads to a more organic and dynamic approach to strategy compared with the traditional approach, which is heavily influenced by the machine metaphor.

The demand-driven business model of eBay fundamentally changes the nature of the pricing system and will revolutionize the way companies (particularly retailers) do business. eBay is a true peer-to-peer model. It facilitates direct exchanges between people who go to its site to list products for sale or to search listings of products for sale. The actual exchange takes place between individuals. Just as the music file-swapping company Napster provides a central file directory that allows individuals to swap songs, eBay provides a central listing that allows individuals to buy and sell merchandise. As with Napster, each network member can act as either distributor or consumer.

In essence, eBay makes its money by providing a technology platform that enables users to interact with each other, and then skims money off every transaction. This model, like the demand-aggregation models of other e-pioneers, moves from a fixed "take it or leave it" price determined by sellers (and based most often on cost) to a variable price that actually reflects the true value to the customer as determined by the customers themselves.

Internet-based alliances

The Net and digital media open up new ways to create wealth. Companies like Shwab, eBay, Cisco, MP3 and Linux have transformed the rules of competition in their industries by making revolutionary offerings to their customers. They did not achieve this alone: combining with like-minded partners with complementary skills was the key. In their book *Digital Capital: harnessing the power of business webs* Don Tapscott, David Ticoll and Alex Lowy call these Internet-based partnerships or alliances "business webs," or "b-webs" for short. A b-web, according to the authors, is "*a distinct system of suppliers, distributors, commerce services providers, infrastructure providers and customers that use the Internet for their primary business communications and transactions.*" Although alliance-based, a b-web typically has an identifiable lead partner who formally orchestrates the group's strategies and processes.

The rise of the Internet, the ever-increasing speed of change, and the complicated networks within which organizations now conduct business have exposed the limitations of strategic models based on the single business unit using linear and static assumptions. As a result, the unit of strategic analysis has moved from the single company or business unit to the "extended enterprise," the network of suppliers, customers, and alliances, which together define an organization's ability to create core competencies and strategic advantage. Competence is now seen most often as a function of the collective knowledge available to the whole system – the enhanced network of suppliers, manufacturers, partners, investors and customers.

The simple conclusion – strategy has an e-dimension

One thing seems certain – the reach of the Internet is bringing more intensified competition just about everywhere. Companies like Valeo and Cemex illustrate well the effect of being able to extend a company's competitive reach globally thanks to the Internet, spreading their costs over a widening market. Does all this mean that business will, after all, be the main beneficiary of both the Internet and new technology more broadly? Maybe not. For although there seems to be plenty of scope for cost-cutting, and even for productivity improvements, neither may end up feeding through into greater profits. It is more likely that greater competition, more transparency, and lower barriers to entry may well ensure that the biggest beneficiaries may ultimately be the consumers.

Technological doors have opened wide to a new global, electronic economy. But the new economy is not built simply on fast distribution of information. There is also a central premise of continuous change which by its nature requires constant improvement and innovation, and these are derived from the minds and imaginations of people. To compete, we have to innovate faster than the next person – who is trying to do the same thing. And of course, the next person could be anywhere, in just about any country in the world.

The Global Dimension

Implications of globalization:

» Your biggest competitor is less likely to be down the road and more likely to be based on another continent.
» Size is not everything.
» Global brands need to adapt to national markets.
» Competitive advantage is wonderful if you have advantages with which to be competitive.
» Removal of barriers does make it a little easier for people in poor countries to compete with those in rich ones.
» Technological revolution makes it easier for poor countries to compete on something approaching equal terms.
» Globalization opens people's minds to an unprecedented range of ideas and influences.
» Importers and exporters have a strong financial interest in a globalized economy.
» Mergers and alliances: the big are getting bigger.
» There are increasing levels of regulation.
» Trade is still predominantly regional.
» Globalization intensifies the need for companies to strive for excellence.

"Globalization is made possible by the active exchange and utilization of information."

Daniel Burrus, Burrus Research Associates Inc.

Globalization, which can be defined as the integration of economic activity across national or regional boundaries, has had a mixed press in recent times: on the one hand resented and denounced, most forcibly through demonstrations like those in Seattle in November 1999 and in Genoa in July 2001; on the other hand seen by some as a desirable opening-up of fresh market places and, in any case, inevitable.

John Micklethwait and Adrian Wooldridge, who both work at *The Economist*, explored the phenomenon of globalization in their recent book *A Future Perfect*, which they wrote with two explicit aims:

"The first is to apply some order to the maelstrom of facts, images and opinions concerning globalization. In part that means unraveling some of the myths that have been built up about it: that it is ushering in an age of global products; that it has killed inflation and changed the rules of economics; that big, local companies will crush their smaller rivals; and that geography means nothing in an age of rootless capitalism. Rather than treat globalization as one great co-ordinated movement – or, even more misleadingly, as an accomplished fact – we will argue that it should be seen as a series of waves, rather like the industrial revolution . . . The second aim . . . is to make [an] intellectual case for globalization. For many economists – perhaps too many – that project is too easy to waste time over. Of course globalization makes sense: it leads to a more efficient use of resources; any student who understands the basic tenets of comparative advantage understands that.

"Though hard to dispute, this argument seems inadequate for two reasons. First, it fails to confront the harsh questions concerning those people who lose on account of globalization, not just economically but socially and culturally. And second, it undersells globalization: the process has not only to do with economic efficiency; it has also to do with freedom. Globalization offers the chance to fulfil (or at least come considerably closer to fulfilling) the goals that classical liberal philosophers first identified several centuries ago and that still underpin Western democracy."

Embracing these two aims, Micklethwait and Wooldridge take us on a global journey, ranging from the shanty towns of Sao Paulo to a London townhouse that has revolutionized the telecommunications industry, and from the borders of Russia to the sex industry in the San Fernando valley. In the course of this journey, they explore some of the central issues at the heart of the globalization debate. Can the nation-state survive the politics of interdependence? Should businesses go global and what are the secrets of business success in a global age? Are we creating a winner-take-all society? What should and what can be done about the losers from globalization?

It is clear then that globalization, both as a process of international integration and of growing interconnection, is not just a business phenomenon, but also a political, social, and cultural one. And it is a continuing phenomenon. Eric Hobsbawm expresses this well in his book *The New Century*:

"We are certainly a single global economy compared with thirty years ago, but we can say with equal certainty that we'll be even more globalized in 2050, and very much more in 2100. Globalization is not the product of a single action, like switching on a light or starting a car engine. It is a historical process that has undoubtedly speeded up enormously in the last ten years, but it is a permanent, constant transformation. It is not at all clear, therefore, at what stage we can say it has reached its final destination and can be considered complete. This is principally because it essentially involves expanding across a globe that is by its very nature varied geographically, climatically, and historically. This reality imposes certain limitations on the unification of the entire planet. However, we are all agreed that globalization, and especially the globalized economy, has made such spectacular progress that today you couldn't talk of an international division of labor as we did before the seventies."

So what are the implications of globalization for anybody involved in formulating or implementing strategy in a business? Here are a selection of factors that company strategists may need to bear in mind, depending on the nature and scope of their enterprise:

» Your biggest competitor is less likely to be down the road and more likely to be based on another continent. Although sometimes, paradoxically, if you remove barriers, the advantages that come from being based in a particular place, like Silicon Valley or Hollywood, can matter more rather than less.

» Size is not everything. The big faceless corporations will not necessarily rule. If anything, globalization tends to help small companies by bringing the world to their door.

» There will be an increasing number of global products but even these global brands will often need to adapt to national markets, and even to micro-markets within the national market. Coca-Cola has had to change its formula just to keep different parts of Japan happy.

» The strong economies retain some advantage. As Micklethwait and Wooldridge have put it, "The doctrine of competitive advantage is wonderful if you have advantages with which to be competitive." Even so, the removal of barriers does make it a little easier for people in poor countries to compete with those in rich ones. Combine this with the spread of management ideas, the flow of capital, and – to recap the e-dimension – the technological revolution that is making computer power ever cheaper, and it does make it easier than ever before for poor people to compete on something approaching equal terms.

» Globalization opens people's minds to an unprecedented range of ideas and influences. Free trade allows ordinary people to buy from whichever company they choose – the inevitable consequence is that customers are going to be presented with constantly increasing choice and, as a result, will get ever more picky. Being adequate at what you do will become an increasingly unsustainable strategy.

» Importers have a strong financial interest in a globalized economy. But so do exporters dependent on imported parts and machinery. Industrialists with interests in ports, shipping, international warehousing, and other aspects of international trade and commerce may also see globalization as beneficial to their sectors of the economy.

» Mergers and alliances on an ever-grander scale are a feature of the global economy. The big are getting bigger. However, despite their market share and continuing growth, the top 200 companies continue to employ only a fraction of the world's workers. In 1999, they employed less than one percent of the world's work force, compared with their 27 percent share of world economic activity. And while corporate profits grew three and a half-fold between 1983 and 1999, the number of people employed by these same companies only increased by 14.4 percent.

» There are increasing levels of regulation for companies to contend with. The refusal by the European Economic Union in July 2001 to countenance the merger of two American companies, General Electric and Honeywell, caused outrage in the United States. All the evidence is that the world's antitrust and financial regulators face a more difficult job than before, but their authority is not obviously less than it was.

Before we get too carried away, let us bear in mind that there are those who remain sceptical about the extent of the impact of globalization. Francis Fukuyama, for one, speaking at a Merrill Lynch Forum in 1998, expressed his doubts: "I think that in many respects, globalization is still superficial. Although there is a great deal of talk about it currently, the underlying truth is that the global economy is still limited. It seems to me that the real layer of globalization is restricted to the capital markets. In most other areas, institutions remain intensely local ... Trade, for example, is still predominantly regional."

Perhaps the heart of Fukuyama's message is that the globalization story is not yet fully played out. Already, though, we can draw some overall conclusions. And a key conclusion for the business strategist is that globalization does not equate to homogenization. As consumers seek more choice, so companies that find themselves stretched to deliver what customers want will fall prey to others that can accommodate their customers' needs.

So perhaps the over-riding impact of globalization on business strategy is that it intensifies the need for companies to strive for excellence. Jack Welch, as ever, stated it succinctly in *Strategy and Business Magazine*, Q2, 1996: "The winning companies in the global competition will be those companies that can put together the best of research, engineering, design, manufacturing, distribution – wherever they can get it, anywhere in the world – and the best of each of these will not come from one country or from one continent."

LET'S STICK TOGETHER: THE IMPORTANCE OF CLUSTERS

In his book *The Competitive Advantage of Nations*, Michael Porter defined clusters as "geographic concentrations of interconnected companies, specialized suppliers, service providers, firms in related industries, and associated institutions in particular fields that compete but also co-operate." Probably the two best-known clusters, and certainly the mostly widely cited, are Silicon Valley and Hollywood.

In a global economy, there is, on the face of it, every opportunity for companies competing in related industries to be based just about anywhere that has reasonable access to the relevant market place. In an interview in 1999, published in the Harvard title *Working Knowledge: A Report on Research at Harvard Business School*, Michael Porter seized on this apparent paradox:

> "In a global economy where it's easy to move goods and information around the world, these things become givens available to any enterprise. As a result, they are no longer a source of competitive advantage. The decisive, enduring advantages, therefore, become unique local centers of innovation for the likes of mutual funds, venture capital, and biotechnology in Greater Boston or aircraft equipment and design, boat and shipbuilding, and metal fabrication in Seattle. The list of clusters goes on and on, both in this country and abroad. With the proximity that clusters provide, companies can do things together without formal ownership or legal relationships. And this kind of flexibility opens up more possibilities for change and dynamism, which are crucial ingredients in a modern economy, where prosperity depends on innovation."

So, it seems, even in an age of globalization, local economic circumstances still matter. Although clusters are most common in the advanced economies, they are also one of the essential steps for countries aiming to move in that direction.

And how are clusters nurtured in emerging nations? In Costa Rica, for instance, with a long history of investing in education, a cluster in information technology began to develop a number of years ago. Porter tells the story: "Eventually [that] convinced Intel to build a plant there.

Related actions followed, including supplier upgrading programs and modernization of the airport. Building a true cluster in Costa Rica will take decades to complete, but I'm confident that it will be sustainable because the country offers some unique qualities that are a source of competitive advantage – among them, the highest computer usage in Latin America. Without these, all the intervention in the world won't help.''

For *A Future Perfect*, John Micklethwait and Adrian Wooldridge spent a long time examining companies that formed part of the Silicon Valley cluster with the goal of pinning down the cultural attributes that have proved vital to the Valley's success. Here are what they termed "the ten habits of highly successful clusters":

A firm belief in meritocracy: the Valley endlessly renews itself by bringing in new brains.

An extremely high tolerance for failure: hardly surprising then that Internet companies gravitated towards Silicon Valley.

Tolerance of treachery: neither secrets nor employees are kept for long, but this is accepted as the inevitable consequence of running talent-intensive businesses.

Collaboration: companies and individuals regularly form short-term alliances.

A penchant for risk: there is an attitude that one winning idea will pay for scores of failures.

Re-investment back into the cluster: unusually, money made in the Valley tends to be ploughed back into the Valley, thus helping to guarantee the continuing health of the cluster.

Enthusiasm for change: companies fear that to get stuck in a rut is to risk ending up dead.

Obsession with the product: this is in part driven by the knowledge that winning products tend to get enormous market shares

Generous opportunity: success is admired and aspired to rather than begrudged.

Strong inclination towards sharing wealth: when Valley firms are sold, the founders more often than not share a sizeable amount of the proceeds with company workers.

The State of the Art

» Strategy as Plan
» Strategy as Ploy
» Strategy as Pattern
» Strategy as Position
» Strategy as Perspective

Strategic Lenses:

Lens 1: A Resource Model of Strategy
Lens 2: Strategy as Simple Rules
Lens 3: Strategy as Alignment
Lens 4: Strategy as Learning Process
Lens 5: Strategy as Dream-weaving
Lens 6: Strategy as an Organic Discipline

» The fundamental of strategy: keeping the customer satisfied
» The future of strategy: strategy as a chaotic discipline

"The sobering truth is that our theories, models, and conventional wisdom combined appear no better at predicting an organization's ability to sustain itself than if we were to rely on random chance."

Richard Pascale, "Managing on the Edge"

"How should companies set about developing the insights that will give them exciting yet practical strategies? The answer is, we don't know."

Andrew Campbell & Marcus Alexander, Ashridge Strategic Management Centre, writing in the Harvard Business Review in November 1997

Our perception of strategy has been changing in recent times. It has traditionally been considered a "hard" discipline with its roots in planning and analysis. However, over the past few years, writers, management theorists, and organizational practitioners have increasingly questioned this model of strategy. Some suggest that the future is to all intents unknowable and that the discipline of strategic planning needs to absorb the implications of this; others propose a "softer", more humanistic perspective on strategic change.

In *Crafting Strategy*, one of the best known articles on strategy in the last 20 years, Henry Mintzberg uses the analogy of the potter's wheel to liken the strategic process to a craft. He argues that strategies need not necessarily be deliberate, but can also emerge through circumstances. In other words, a strategy can *form* rather than need to be *formulated*. While strategy is a word that is usually associated with the future, its link to the past is no less central. Like potters at the wheel, organizations must make sense of the past if they hope to manage the future. Only by coming to understand the patterns that form in their own behavior do they get to know their capabilities and their potential.

The "hard/soft" debate continues to this day. In an article in *Gemini Magazine*, in Autumn 1993, entitled "Bridging the Hard-Soft Gap," Bob Kaplan (inventor of the balanced scorecard) and Chris Argyris (a leading authority on organizational behavior) attempted to integrate the hard and soft aspects of management theory through a discussion centred on Activity Based Costing (ABC).

The word "strategy" has been used implicitly in different ways, even if it has traditionally been defined in only one. Explicit recognition of multiple definitions can help people to maneuver through this difficult field. In his book *The Strategic Process*, Henry Mintzberg provides five definitions of strategy:

» *Strategy as Plan*: Strategies have two essential characteristics: they are made in advance of the actions to which they apply, and they are developed consciously and purposefully.

» *Strategy as Ploy*: A strategy can be a ploy too, really just a specific maneuver intended to outwit an opponent or competitor.

» *Strategy as Pattern*: If strategies can be intended (whether as general plans or specific ploys), they can also be realized. In other words, defining strategy as plan is not sufficient; we also need a definition that encompasses the resulting behavior: Strategy is a pattern – specifically, a pattern in a stream of actions. Strategy is consistency in behavior, whether or not intended. Whereas plans are intended strategy, patterns are realized strategy; from this we can distinguish deliberate strategies, where intentions that existed previously were realized, and emergent strategies where patterns developed in the absence of intentions, or despite them.

» *Strategy as Position*: Strategy is a position – specifically a means of locating an organization in an "environment". By this definition, strategy becomes the mediating force, or "match", between organization and environment, that is, between the internal and the external context.

» *Strategy as Perspective*: Strategy is a perspective, with its content consisting of an ingrained way of perceiving the world. Strategy in this respect is to the organization what personality is to the individual. It is important here that strategy is a perspective shared by members of an organization, through their intentions and their actions. In this context, we are entering the realm of the collective mind – individuals united by common thinking and/or behavior.

We know that strategy provides a means by which organizations and individuals can examine their internal and external worlds. As the business world has lost confidence in the traditional strategic perspective that the future is predictable, relatively slow to unfold, and therefore readily manageable, there is no longer a sense that there is a one best way to "do" strategy.

As we have seen, Mintzberg has suggested that there are many ways of perceiving the strategic process. This is important, because the way we perceive has a deep influence on the way we behave. An example of this is the *Pygmalion* effect. In George Bernard Shaw's play of that name, Professor Henry Higgins makes a wager that he can take a Cockney flower-seller from Covent Garden Market in London and teach her to speak proper English and pass herself off as a duchess. The girl, Eliza Doolittle, manages to transform herself in the eyes of the world, and everyone does treat her as a titled lady – but she remains a flower-seller as far as Higgins is concerned.

In the business world, the expectations we have of the strategic process shape what we believe strategy is capable of delivering for us, and what we believe what we can get out of it. These expectations are diverse because there are a number of "lenses" through which we can view strategy. Here are some of them:

LENS 1: A RESOURCE MODEL OF STRATEGY

One of the most common ways of looking at strategy today is through the lens of resources. The resource-based view of the organization (RBV) combines the internal analysis of key capabilities and core competencies with the external analysis of the industry and competitive environment. It sees capabilities and resources as the heart of a company's competitive position. Resources are defined as the firm's special assets, skills and capabilities.

The RBV sees companies as very different collections of physical and intangible assets and capabilities. No two companies are alike because no two companies have undergone the same set of experiences, acquired the same assets and skills, or built the same organizational cultures. These assets and capabilities determine how efficiently and effectively a company performs its functional activities. The resource-based view of strategy holds that competitive advantage, whatever its source, can ultimately be attributed to the ownership of a valuable resource that enables a company to perform activities better or more cheaply than competitors.

Superior performance is based on developing a *competitively distinct* set of resources which are deployed in a well-conceived strategy. Resources include the following:

» *Physical resources*, which include location, the regulatory framework, and other physical factors.
» *Intangible resources*, which include brand names, technological know-how, and other non-physical assets.
» *Organizational capabilities*, which include the routines and processes embedded within an organization, and the culture of the organization itself.

Resources cannot be evaluated in isolation because their value is determined in the interplay with market forces.

The dynamic interplay of three fundamental market forces determines the value of a resource or capability:

» *Demand*: meeting customer needs through competitive superiority.
» *Scarcity*: the supply factor, which includes consideration of whether the resource is inimitable, substitutable and durable.
» *Appropriability*: the ownership of the profits.

The value of a resource depends on a number of factors. David J. Collis and Cynthia A. Montgomery, writing in *Harvard Business Review* in July/August 1995 under the title "Competing on Resources: Strategy in the 1990s," put forward five tests to determine the value of a resource.

» *Inimitability*. Is the resource hard to copy? This is the heart of value creation because it limits competition. It can take several forms: *Physical uniqueness*: many managers believe that their resources fall into this category, but on close inspection few actually do. *Path dependency*: all that has happened along the path taken in resource accumulation (including brand building). *Causal ambiguity*: It is often impossible to disentangle what the valuable resource is or how to re-create it. Causally ambiguous resources are often organizational capabilities, which exist as a complex web of social interactions and may even depend critically on particular key individuals. *Economic deterrence*: Barriers to entry: large investment can only support one profitable organization in the market.
» *Durability*. How quickly does the resource depreciate? In reality, the value of almost all resources depreciates quickly.

» *Appropriability*. Who captures the value that the resources create? Value is subject to bargaining among a host of players, including customers, distributors, suppliers, and employees.

» *Substitutability*. Can a unique resource be trumped by another resource?

» *Competitive superiority*. Resource values are relative to those of competitors. Core competence has too often become a "feel good" exercise that no-one fails. Core competence should not be an internal assessment of which activity, of all activities, a company performs best. It should be a harsh external assessment of what it does better than competitors, for which the term distinctive competence is more appropriate. This requires capabilities and resources to be desegregated and a holistic viewpoint to be taken of how they fit together synergistically.

LENS 2: STRATEGY AS SIMPLE RULES

Expanding our horizons, shifting our perspective, is rarely easy because it involves risk, and the decision to take this risk, to step out of our comfort zone, implies a deep, personal commitment to change. It needs to be a conscious decision, which recognizes that the future is never completely knowable, acknowledges the vulnerability involved, and recognizes the trust that is implicit in such a decision. So, while strategy may be a state of mind, it is also a matter for the heart. Without this commitment, strategy remains a cerebral matter; interesting perhaps, but unlikely to change much of anything.

Like all effective strategies, strategy as simple rules is about being different. But that difference does not arise from tightly-linked activity systems or leveraged core competencies, as in traditional strategies. It arises from focusing on key strategic processes and developing simple rules that shape those processes. When a pattern emerges from the processes – a pattern that creates network effects or economies of scale or scope – the result can be a long-term competitive advantage like the ones Intel and Microsoft achieved for over a decade. More often, the competitive advantage is short term.

These key strategic processes are designed to place the company in a position where managers can pursue the most promising opportunities. They are also essential to provide discipline in turbulent, high-velocity markets. Simple rules, which grow out of experience, fall into five broad categories: how-to rules, boundary conditions, priority rules, timing rules, and exit rules. The following table defines these categories (Table 6.1).

LENS 3: STRATEGY AS ALIGNMENT

Leaders cannot change organizations on their own. Successful change depends on bringing people along with you. In other words, aligning the personal vision of individuals to the wider vision of the organization itself. This is far more than a grudging acceptance of organizational reality by employees; it implies a deep sense of emotional commitment to making change happen. For this to occur, individuals must see the shared vision as an extension of their personal vision rather than a series of sacrifices to their personal interests. Peter Senge, Director for the Centre of Organizational Learning at MIT's Sloan School of Management, talks of the process as "lining up all the arrows". This involves making sure that the energy of individuals is flowing in the same direction so that it complements itself and contributes to the overall vision of the organization. In this sense, alignment is all about freeing the flow, so that individual energies can be liberated in the service of a common objective. Senge, in his book *The Fifth Discipline*, observes:

> "In a corporation, a shared vision changes people's relationship with the company. It is no longer 'their company'; it becomes 'our company.' A shared vision is the first step in allowing people who mistrusted each other to begin to work together. It creates a common identity."

Alignment is an exceptionally difficult concept to grasp because few of us have direct experience of it in real life. What experience we have is normally found outside our working life; playing team sports, playing music in a band, as part of a charitable group, or where we work with like-minded individuals engaged in our favourite hobby or pastime. It is something we experience in a feeling sense that generates excitement, passion and a sense of "wholeness." These are times when we feel that it is a pleasure to be alive. It is often marked by a lack of awareness of

Table 6.1 Simple rules of strategy.

Type	Purpose	Example
How-to rules	They spell out key features of how a process is executed – "What makes our process unique?"	Akamai's rules for customer service process: staff must consist of technical gurus, every question must be answered on the first call or e-mail, and R & D staff must rotate through customer service.
Boundary rules	They focus managers on which opportunities can be pursued, and which are outside the pale.	Cisco's early acquisition rule: companies to be acquired must have no more than 75 employees, 75% of whom are engineers.
Priority rules	They help managers to rank the accepted opportunities.	Intel's rule for allocating manufacturing capacity: allocation is based on a product's gross margin.
Timing rules	They synchronize managers with the pace of emerging opportunities and other parts of the company.	Nortel's rules for product development: project teams must know when a product has to be delivered to the leading customer to win, and product development time must be less than 18 months.
Exit rules	They help managers decide when to pull out of yesterday's opportunities.	Oticon's rule for pulling the plug on projects in development: if a key team member – manager or not – chooses to leave the project for another within the company, the project is killed.

Source; "Strategy as simple rules", Kathleen M.Eisenhardt and Donald N. Sull, *Harvard Business Review*, January 2001 the passing of time; we "wake up" and can be surprised to discover that a whole day has somehow passed.

Transferring this alignment to an organizational setting is far more challenging. Building a shared sense of vision is predicated on the other factors in the crucible of change; the ability of a leader to crystallize the vision, the presence of a safe and trusting environment within which individual creativity can flourish, and the willingness of individuals to take personal responsibility for achieving the organizational vision, either on their own, or as part of a wider team. However, when shared vision is genuinely achieved, the effect on an organization can be dramatic. Angeles Arrien, an anthropologist, explains what happens when geese fly in formation:

> "As each bird flaps its wings it creates an uplift for the bird behind. By travelling on the thrust of one another they create 71 per cent greater flying range than when a bird flies alone. When the lead goose gets tired, it rotates back into formation and another goose takes over the lead. The geese flying at the back honk from behind to encourage those up in front to keep up their speed."
>
> *Quoted by Kate Hall, in "The trials of community life", Kindred Spirit Magazine, Spring 1996*

LENS 4: STRATEGY AS LEARNING PROCESS

For most of us, answering the basic questions proves extraordinarily difficult. Few of us spend much time considering the fundamental life issues that lie below these questions despite, or perhaps because of, the fact that we lead very busy lives. Of course, all of us would *like* to spend more time thinking about these matters; it is just that there never seems enough time to do so! We are consumed by what Sogyal Rinpoche calls "active laziness" in *The Tibetan Book of Living and Dying*:

> "Naturally there are different species of laziness: Eastern and Western. The Eastern style is like the one practised to perfection in India. It consists of hanging out all day in the sun, doing nothing, avoiding any kind of work or useful activity, drinking cups of tea, listening to Hindi film music blaring on the radio, and gossiping

with friends. Western laziness is quite different. It consists of cramming our lives with compulsive activity, so that there is no time at all to confront the real issues."

The exercise *is* hard because it touches on the raw stuff of life and demands high levels of awareness, honesty and humility in responding to it. Indeed, that is exactly why this simple strategic framework is so powerful. Look closely at many models of change, from psychotherapy to soldiers communicating in battle, and you will detect the same fundamental structure.

Just as the exercise is difficult for us as individuals, so it is even more difficult for organizations because it requires large groups of individuals to share a common sense of purpose and direction. As a result, many organizations shy away from seeking the deeper meaning of these questions altogether and take an imperious approach to decision-making, or take cover behind the multitude of models and analytical techniques that exist for looking at performance, industry structure, customers, markets and competition.

This reticence to look at deeper issues has traditionally been more prevalent in Western organizations than in their Japanese competitors, one reason for the successful rise of many Japanese companies in the 1980s. So it is that successful strategies often prove elusive despite (or perhaps because of) abundant resources and "deep organizational pockets." Learning to look at the deeper issues underlying strategy is like learning to draw. As Kimon Nicolaides describes it:

"Learning to draw is really a matter of learning to see – to see correctly – and that means a good deal more than merely looking with the eye."
Quoted by Betty Edwards in "Drawing on the Right Side of the Brain"

Thus, strategy can be summarized as the process of learning to see the place that the organization holds in the world, its purpose, the human needs that it exists to fulfil, and how these needs are likely to change in the future (whether customers can articulate these future needs or not). This is simply not possible without reflection on the deepest nature of things.

LENS 5: STRATEGY AS DREAM-WEAVING

John Stopford, Professor of International Business at London Business School, is one of a number of authors who stress that strategy without passion and vision from the people creating and implementing it is nothing. As a result, he argued in an article "Strategists as dream-weavers" in the *Harvard Business Review* that dreams need to be at the front and the center of the strategy-making process. Three aspects of the new business environment are driving this change:

» The extraordinarily rapid decline in transaction costs in markets around the world. As a result, many of the traditional advantages of scale are disappearing, allowing small companies to compete with the giants. Competitors are emerging from all quarters to challenge the established order and incumbents need to improve their peripheral vision to get early warning of threats. Then – very rapidly – they need to innovate. It is this need for quick action and reaction that thwarts the traditional strategy-making process.

» The Internet has vastly increased the supply of information available to organizations. Since the networked economy has effectively broadened the base of organizational intelligence, it no longer makes sense to restrict strategic dialogue to a few executives at the top; the top-down process ignores valuable data, ideas and energy. It is no longer good enough to rely solely on *stretch* targets set at the top. It is often much more productive to let individuals and teams translate the organizational dream or vision into a *reach* target that they impose on themselves.

» There is increasing competition among business models resulting in strategy being as much about alternative ideas and business models as about access to resources. Today, business models, like their underlying technologies, are changing at an increasing pace. In previous eras, innovative strategies involved largely one-off efforts that relied on controlling physical assets. Now that the key organizational asset is ideas, competitive advantage can be brief, and companies must push ahead with new approaches to the market place if they are to grow, or even survive. As John Stopford puts it, "to change a business model once is hard enough; to do so repeatedly is the frontier challenge."

The need to widen the strategic net is critical. Andy Grove, former CEO of Intel, has said that companies do not need radical strategies but they do need to radically broaden their process for getting to the winning strategy. This is particularly important in a networked economy, which is causing radical changes to the location of value added in most industries.

John Stopford concludes that today's strategists would do well to adopt entrepreneurial attitudes. When companies start to transform themselves, no one knows for sure how they will reach their ambitious goals; the means to the end are discovered along the way. The same is true for entrepreneurs, whose goals usually far exceed the available resources. Entrepreneurs often state their goals in emotional terms that lend new meaning and dignity to the work required. They do not just have goals, they have dreams that are necessarily irrational – in that the logic of today's market tells them they cannot do it! Strategy-making in the digital age requires this kind of entrepreneurial mind-set if it is to command the energy and dedication of all concerned.

LENS 6: STRATEGY AS AN ORGANIC DISCIPLINE

Current writers and thinkers in strategy have taken up the call to arms. Kathleen Eisenhardt, for example, talks of strategy as "structured chaos" and brings in biological models such as *co-evolution* to help explain the complex process of gaining market advantage by building a web of shifting alliances and partnerships. In this model, managers continually change the web of collaborative links in response to changing market circumstances. This is a much more fluid view of strategy than the traditional model and one better suited to the needs of the modern world. It also highlights important aspects of strategy that can sometimes be counter-intuitive, for example the need for partners (whether internal or external) *both* to collaborate and compete, and the need for the organization to reward business unit managers on the basis both of collaboration *and* self-interest.

THE FUNDAMENTAL OF STRATEGY: KEEPING THE CUSTOMER SATISFIED

Whichever lens a company chooses to apply, it will almost inevitably end up back with the customer. Both traditional and new strategic models, if they are worth a pinch of salt, are about being different in the eyes of the customer and adding a unique benefit to those customers.

It has long been an axiom that businesses should be "customer-facing," responsive to the real needs of customers (even when customers may be unaware of their broader needs or unable to express them at a conscious level). It is only recently, however, that technology has begun to empower the customer and move him or her into the very center of the business model. Many new models of strategy acknowledge this critical change by renewing their emphasis on customer-centered business models. C.K. Prahalad, Professor of Business at the University of Michigan Business School, and his colleague Venkatram Ramaswamy, Associate Professor of Marketing, for example, talk in terms of customers as active co-developers of business value through the creation of personalized experiences, rather than simply passive buyers of standardized goods and services.

In the new economy, the relationship between customer and company moves beyond the acknowledgement of the customer as a person with individual tastes and expectations (which, in itself, implies cultivating trust and relationship) to recognizing each customer as part of a greater social and cultural fabric, which includes the organization and its key partners. Similarly, the organization begins to take a broader view of the development of its core competencies, moving from a company-centered view to one based on an enhanced network.

ONE VIEW OF THE FUTURE OF STRATEGY: STRATEGY AS A CHAOTIC DISCIPLINE

There is no real knowing where strategy might be heading over the next few years. As movie mogul Sam Goldwyn once famously said: "It's difficult to make predictions, especially about the future." However, there is a growing body of opinion within the strategy field that the world is essentially unpredictable and the future inherently unknowable because events are chaotic by nature.

Chaos theory is a broad body of work which looks at the under-lying behavior of systems which are governed by simple physical laws, but where events appear to be so unpredictable that they might as well be random. In this sense, *chaos* does not mean absolute muddle and confusion; it is the study of the complex relationships that underlie the everyday systems that we observe in the real world. In reality, these relationships are non-linear and dynamic, making them extraordinarily complex because a single action can have a host of different effects, causing the surface links between cause and effect to disappear (or be hidden within a more complex system). Moreover, we cannot meaningfully approximate these relationships using the kind of linear assumptions with which we feel comfortable. As James Gleick, the author of *Chaos: Making a New Science* (Penguin Books, New York 1987) writes in the prolog of his book:

"Watch two bits of foam flowing side by side at the bottom of a waterfall. What can you guess about how close they were at the top? Nothing. As far as standard physics was concerned, God might just as well have taken all those water molecules under the table and shuffled them personally ... Tiny differences in input (can) quickly become overwhelming differences in output – a phenomenon given the name 'sensitive dependence on initial condition.' In weather, for example, this translates into what is only half-jokingly known as the Butterfly Effect – the notion that a butterfly stirring the air today in Peking can transform storm systems next month in New York."

The greatest contribution of chaos theory is the realization that even the simplest systems are now seen to create extraordinarily difficult problems of predictability. This represents nothing less than a paradigm shift because it challenges our implicit assumption that we live in a stable world where instability is the exception.

The truth is that we live in a chaotic universe ruled by entropy, the inexorable tendency towards greater and greater disorder. In these circumstances it is no surprise that long-term planning has been notoriously inaccurate in predicting the future. Indeed, detailed planning systems, and the econometric models that sometimes underlie them, cannot be effective because we simply cannot look with any certainty into the future. As James Gleick points out:

"In practice, econometric models proved dismally blind to what the future would bring, but many people who should have known better acted as though they believed in the results."

Strategy is adapting by borrowing concepts originating in the sciences, notably both physics and biology. This strategic lens stresses adaptability, flexibility and speed of change, rather than static positioning and long-term competitive advantage. It is not just "running faster" but "thinking faster" that matters.

Prahalad and Ramaswamy talk of the need to prepare the organization for the emerging multi-channel world which will place a high premium on organizational flexibility:

"In fact, no part of the company – a single salesperson or an entire business unit – will be able to assume that its role in the organization is stable. As business models are revised and new challenges and opportunities emerge, the organization will constantly have to reconfigure its resources – its people, machines, infrastructure, and capital. Managers have to create 'Velcro organizations', in which resources can be reconfigured seamlessly and with as little effort as possible – as in Velcro hooking and unhooking."

Perhaps there are still organizations for whom the future is clearly laid out and whose place in the world is assured. But their numbers are declining rapidly – many have learned to their cost that nothing can be taken for granted. For most of those who work in or with organizations, the challenge is to throw away the strategic rule-book and focus instead on capturing unanticipated, fleeting opportunities in order to succeed. In traditional strategy, advantage has comes from exploiting resources or stable market positions. In future strategy, advantage will come from successfully exploiting these fleeting opportunities.

To achieve this, an organization will have to have unprecedented levels of flexibility This in turn is likely to impose psychological and emotional traumas on its employees, since there are limits to an individual's ability to respond to rapid external changes. Paradoxically, this increases the importance of maintaining a stable center, based on a strong set of organizational values.

AND FOR NOW: STAY VIGILANT

In their book *Profit from the Core*, Chris Zook and James Allen suggest the following ten questions that management teams should periodically ask themselves about their companies as they find themselves in an almost infinite variety of strategic situations.

What is the most tightly-defined profitable core of our business, and is it gaining or losing strength?

What defines the boundaries of the business that we are competing for, and where are those boundaries going to shift in the future?

Are there new competitors currently at the fringe of our business who pose potential longer-term threats to the core?

Are we certain that we are achieving the full strategic and operating potential of our core business; the "hidden value" of the core?

What is the full set of potential adjacencies to our core business and possible adjacency moves (single or multiple moves)? Are we looking at these in a planned, logical sequence or piecemeal?

What is our point of view on the future of the industry? As a team, do we have consensus? How is this point of view shaping our adjacency strategy and point of arrival?

Should major new growth initiatives be pursued inside, next to, or outside the core? How should we decide?

Is industry turbulence changing the fundamental source of future competitive advantage? How? Through new models? New segments? New competitors? And what are we monitoring on a regular basis?

Are organizational enablers and inhibitors to growth in the right balance for the needed change?

What are the guiding strategic principles that should apply consistently to all of our major strategic and operating decisions?

There may well be other key questions that apply to your particular company in your particular industry at this particular time. But being able to address the questions posed by Zook and Allen will put you in a stronger position than most of your competitors.

Good luck!

Strategy in Practice

- » Encyclopaedia Britannica: a demonstration of how quickly the new economics of information have changed the rules of competition.
- » Pleasant Company: creating a total shopping experience for which customers are willing to pay a premium price.
- » Sears: change in the logic and culture of a business.
- » Seven-Eleven Japan: highly effective use of technology combined with cautious management.
- » The Natural Step: creating a shared sense of purpose and vision.
- » Vermeer Technologies: start-ups and buyouts – the rock and roll of strategy.
- » Coda: Garth Brooks Case Study.

"There is nothing more difficult to take in hand, more perilous to conduct, or more uncertain in its success, than to take the lead in the introduction of a new order of things."

Machiavelli

"From the pain come the dream
   From the dream come the vision
   From the vision come the people
   And from the people come the power
   From this power come the change"
   Peter Gabriel, "14 Black Paintings" from the album Us, Real World Records, 1992

Strategy has sometimes been described as one percent theory and ninety nine percent implementation. In order to achieve its strategic goals and objectives, an organization often needs not only a formal plan for implementation of its strategy, but also the capability to move a large body of people from one attitude to another. As we have seen, this implies that the strategic process is rooted in both an awareness of current reality and a powerful vision of what the organization is trying to create. Organizations that successfully transform themselves communicate a very clear vision about what they are, what they want to achieve, and what part they play in the wider world. It is this powerful sense of vision that anchors the change process.

Change has always been with us, although it is only comparatively recently that the notion of change management has been elevated to an important business concept. This clearly reflects the increasingly turbulent business environment; scarcely a day goes by without a major organization re-inventing itself, or otherwise embarking upon a path of transformational change (whether through total quality, process redesign, downsizing or good old-fashioned restructuring initiatives). Over the last decade, radical change programmes have spread rapidly from the private sector to the public sector, voluntary bodies, charitable organizations and, inevitably, into our personal lives. It is probably not surprising, therefore, that organizations have turned their attention to the process of change itself and how best to motivate their people to make the desired level of change.

Most of us fear change. Rather than *managing* change, it is probably more correct to say that we *cope* with change, we *adapt* to it as best we can and, if we are fortunate, we turn it to our advantage. In reality, "managing" the process of change is an illusion. It suggests that we can control or limit the effects of outside events, which are, in the short term, often beyond our control. More seriously, at a deeper level, it ignores our part in creating those events in the first place. Our best organizations do not manage changes thrust upon them, they are instrumental in creating those changes. They recognize their place as co-creators of their destiny.

There is no magic template for our actions, which will depend on the complex inter-relationships between the factors influencing events. Peter Stebel, professor of strategy and change management at IMD, Lausanne, puts the point more bluntly:

> "Those who pretend that the same kind of change medicine can be applied no matter what the context are either naive or charlatans."
>
> *"Managing change", Mastering Management Series (Part 16), Financial Times (1996)*

In this chapter, we shall look at a number of organizations and how they tackled – with varying levels of success – challenges facing their businesses. Each case study will be followed by a brief analysis of key lessons or insights to be drawn.

ENCYCLOPAEDIA BRITANNICA

The organization

The *Encyclopaedia Britannica* was founded in 1768 in Edinburgh, Scotland, by Colin Macfarquhar, a printer, and Andrew Bell, an engraver. Now headquartered in Chicago, Illinois, Encyclopaedia Britannica Inc. and Britannica.com Inc. describe themselves as leading providers of learning and knowledge products.

The story

Between 1990 and 1997, hardback sales of the Encyclopaedia Britannica more than halved. During the same period, sales of CD-ROMs blossomed. When Microsoft launched Encarta, it must have seemed like a toy to Britannica's executives. Britannica's intellectual material was far superior to Encarta, whose content was derived from an encyclopaedia traditionally sold at low cost in supermarkets. However, what the Britannica team failed to understand was that parents had bought their copy of the encyclopaedia because they wanted to "do the right thing" for their children. In the 1990s, parents "did the right thing" by buying a computer. As far as the customer is concerned, Encarta is a near perfect substitute for Britannica.

Add to the equation the enormous cost advantage enjoyed by Encarta, which can be produced for less than $2 a copy, compared with around $300 to produce a set of Britannica, and the recipe for Britannica's downfall was complete.

Analysis

The story of Britannica is more than a parable about the dangers of complacency, it is a demonstration of how quickly the new economics of information have changed the rules of competition. Intriguingly, Britannica has been trying since 1997 to rebuild its business around the Internet.

These days, the company has set its sights on making full use of all new media, including wireless, to make rich information available to people wherever they need it. The company is also actively syndicating some of its more popular features throughout the Internet, making Britannica information more widely accessible. In 2001 BritannicaSchool.com makes its debut as a broad educational service that combines high-quality reference materials with electronic curriculum programs that make learning both engaging and enjoyable.

PLEASANT COMPANY

The organization

Pleasant Company was founded in 1986 by Pleasant T. Rowland, a former educator and publisher of educational materials. Since that time, the company has sold more than 61 million books and five million dolls to a nation-wide audience of girls. According to the company website, "Pleasant Company's products aim to enrich the lives of American girls by fostering pride in the traditions of growing up female in America and celebrating the lifestyle of girls today." Mattel, Inc., the world's leading toy-maker, acquired Pleasant Company in 1998. Pleasant Company continues to operate as an independent subsidiary out of its main headquarters in Middleton, Wisconsin.

The story

As goods and services become increasingly "commoditized," the experience that the customer enjoys while purchasing those goods and services begins to matter far more. In a world where competitive offerings are increasingly undifferentiated, companies are looking to add value by staging experiences. An experience occurs when a company uses services as the stage – and goods as props – for engaging individuals in a way that creates a memorable event. And while experiences have always been at the heart of the entertainment business, any company stages an experience when it engages customers in a personal, memorable way.

American Girl, part of the Pleasant Company, is a practical example of this phenomenon taking place. It is a branded doll emporium based in Chicago which has been taking the world by storm. The store has achieved a synergy between product range and its environment to create a total shopping experience that customers are willing to pay a premium price for.

Analysis

It is a basic tenet in retailing today that the experience of the customer matters as much, if not more, than the purchase of the product itself (provided that quality and service deliverables match or exceed industry standards). American Girl is one of a number of retailers who have developed customer propositions with a higher experience/leisure content, and who are now out-performing the market. Alternatively, are they simply fortunate to benefit from significant structural and economic shifts in the economy?

Crispin Tweddell, Chairman of Piper Private Equity, argues that there is a well-defined relationship between the entertainment/leisure content of a retail offer and its profitability. Bluewater, which is Europe's largest shopping destination based in Kent in Southern England (the term *shopping center* is now avoided by retailers), takes this concept one stage further with "guests" being treated to a full leisure experience by their "hosts."

SEARS

The organization

The company's history dates back to the 1880s, when Richard Sears was an agent of the Minneapolis and St. Louis railway station in North Redwood, Minnesota. Sears' job as station agent left him plenty of spare time, so he sold lumber and coal to local residents on the side to make extra money. Sears set up a mail order business in the 1890s. The company opened its first retail store in 1925; numbers rapidly grew and by 1997 there were over 800 stores.

Today, the company's mission statement is: Sears: a compelling place to shop, to work, and to invest.

The story

In 1992 Sears announced it would again reshape the company to give it greater strength and marketing focus and to give its shareholders a better return on investment.

As part of this restructuring, the Sears Merchandise Group, reorganized around its apparel, home and automotive business, closed many of its under-performing department stores as well as its specialty stores. Its unprofitable catalog merchandise distribution operations also were closed in 1993, leaving a smaller – but successful – direct-response business.

Led by CEO Arthur Martinez, a group of more than 100 top-level Sears executives spent three years rebuilding the company around its customers. In rethinking what Sears was and what it wanted to become, these managers developed a business model of the company – the employee-customer-profit model – and an accompanying measurement system that tracks success from management behavior through employee attitudes to customer satisfaction and financial performance.

More background detail is given in the article "The employee-customer-profit chain at Sears," by Anthony J. Rucci, Steven P. Kirn, and Richard T. Quinn in *Harvard Business Review* January/February 1998.

Analysis

Over the past five years, Sears has radically changed the way it does business and has dramatically improved its financial results. But Sears' transformation was more than a change in marketing strategy. It was also a change in the logic and culture of the business. The company has been rebuilt around its customers using a business model and accompanying performance measures that track success through employee attitudes to customer satisfaction and financial performance. One problem for Sears was measuring such soft data as customer satisfaction. However, by means of an ongoing process of data collection, analysis, modelling and experimentation, Sears not only achieved this but also changed the way in which managers think and behave. This cultural change is now spreading throughout the company.

SEVEN-ELEVEN JAPAN

The organization

Founded in 1973, Seven-Eleven Japan opened in first store in Tokyo the following year. The company established Japan's first true convenience store franchise chain with the stated goal of setting out to "modernize and revitalize small and medium-sized retailers," and to achieve "mutual prosperity." According to its website, the company, in partnership with its member stores and customers, "is committed to continue taking on new and exciting challenges under the motto of 'Responding to change and strengthening fundamentals' so that our convenience stores will always be enjoyed by the people we serve."

As at December 31, 2000, the company had a network of 21,142 stores in 19 regional districts around the world. Early in 2001, Seven-Eleven lifted the title of biggest retailer in Japan from Daiei, a troubled supermarket giant. Unlike Daiei, and a host of others, Seven-Eleven has defied a stumbling economy to increase sales by 4% and profits by 15% in the year to the end of February 2001. Its pre-tax profits last year were more than double those of its nearest rival.

The story

Seven-Eleven has achieved notable success using the Internet, with its e-strategy based mainly around proprietary systems. In the main, it has used the Internet to talk to its retail customers, rather than to run its core business. In Japan, it is one of the companies most admired for the effective use of electronic communications.

By the mid-1980s, it had already replaced old-fashioned cash registers with electronic point-of-sale systems that monitored customer purchases. By 1992, it had overhauled its information-technology systems four times.

In 1995, before the Internet wave had reached Japan to any degree, the company went for a new system based around proprietary – but barely-tested let alone proven – technology.

It worked, and it gave Seven-Eleven four big advantages:

» The first was in its ability to track customer needs at a time when deregulation was making shoppers more picky. According to Makoto Usui, who heads the information-systems department at Seven-Eleven:

"We believed that the nature of competition was changing. Instead of pushing products on to customers, companies were being pulled by customer needs. In this environment, the battleground was at the stores themselves – the interface between businesses and customers."

"Over the counter e-commerce", The Economist, May 26, 2001

» The company collects sales information from every store three times a day, and analyzes it in roughly 20 minutes. As a result, it has bang-up-to-date information about which goods or packaging appeal to customers.

» The technology helps Seven-Eleven to predict daily trends, particularly important as customers become more fickle and product cycles are shortening. It does this partly by monitoring the weather, a critical factor in predicting food purchases.

» The company's technology has vastly improved the efficiency of its supply chain. Orders flow quickly.

Analysis

Much of Seven-Eleven's success can obviously be attributed to its highly effective use of new technology. It pioneered many techniques for using the Internet that remain state of the art to this day.

Another reason is the company's generally cautious management. While rivals expanded, in retrospect, recklessly over the past decade, and then had to announce the closure of hundreds of stores, Seven-Eleven took the view that it would stop opening new stores if sales at existing ones declined sharply. As a result, Seven-Eleven's finances are extremely and largely debt-free.

THE NATURAL STEP

The organization

The Natural Step (TNS) is a non-profit environmental education organization working to build an ecologically and economically sustainable society. The Natural Step offers a framework that is based on science and serves as a compass for businesses, communities, academia, government entities and individuals working to redesign their activities to become more sustainable. Today, TNS has offices in the Australia, Canada, Japan, New Zealand, South Africa, Sweden, the United Kingdom, and the United States.

The stated purpose of TNS is: "To develop and share a common framework comprised of easily understood, scientifically-based principles that can serve as a compass to guide society towards a just and sustainable future."

The story

In Sweden, a group of professional associations, involving some 10,000 people, formed a large-scale social and environmental movement called The Natural Step. They co-operate together on projects that work towards developing a sustainable society. Karl-Henrik Robèrt describes how sustainability provides a shared sense of purpose that binds the associate members together allowing them to create large-scale change:

"What binds (us) together is a collective understanding of the larger system of which we are a part. A system is like a tree – the trunk and the branches are the underlying principles that give form and structure to the system, while the leaves represent the various efforts we can take to meet the principles.

"The various associations – the engineers and scientists, doctors and lawyers – are each operating as the leaves, providing input from their background, while the trunk provides an overarching unity to our work."

"The Natural Step: a framework for large-scale change", The Systems Thinker, October 1995

The Natural Step framework helps individuals and organizations address key environmental issues from a systems perspective, reduce the use of natural resources, develop new technologies, and facilitate better communications among employees and members. It gives people a common language and guiding principles to help to change existing practices and to decrease their impact on the environment. The system conditions have been used as a shared mental model for problem-solving, for the development of consensus documents (e.g. sustainable practices with regard to metals, energy, agriculture, and forestry), to structure institutional scientific work at universities, in course curriculums for the teaching of students, and by business corporations, municipalities and other organizations as an instrument for strategic planning towards sustainability.

Analysis

It is the ability of an organization to create a shared sense of purpose and vision that enables large numbers of people to work together in a co-ordinated way. True vision occurs only when an organization really understands where it wants to go and this aspiration becomes its *primary organizing principle*.

TNS encourages dialogue and consensus-building, a key process of learning organizations. The Natural Step Framework is based on systems thinking, focusing on first-order principles at the beginning of cause/effect relationships.

VERMEER TECHNOLOGIES

The organization

Founded in April 1994 by Dr Charles H. Ferguson and Randy Forgaard, Vermeer Technologies Inc. pioneered the development of powerful, easy-to-use World Wide Web authoring tools that allow end users and professionals to publish on the web without programming. The company's first product, FrontPage, enabled virtually any company to gain the business benefits of web publishing quickly and easily.

The story

REDMOND, Wash. – January 16, 1996 – Microsoft Corp. today announced the acquisition of Vermeer Technologies Inc., a pioneer of visual, standards-based Web publishing tools based in Cambridge, Mass. Vermeer's flagship software application, FrontPage^{TM}, is a critically acclaimed tool for easily creating and managing rich Web documents without programming. FrontPage will become a key component of Microsoft's strategy to provide a full range of tools that put the power of Web publishing, for both the Internet and intranets, in the hands of the broadest range of computer users.

"Millions of productivity-applications users want an easier way to participate in the excitement and enhanced productivity of the Web," said Bill Gates, chairman and CEO of Microsoft. "Vermeer's FrontPage fills the wide gap between simple HTML page editors and high-end, professional Web publishing systems available today.

"Access to Microsoft's resources and channel partnerships will allow us to realize our vision of 'Webtop publishing' on a broader scale," said John Mandile, Vermeer's president and chief executive officer. Vermeer coined the phrase 'Webtop publishing' to define the process of creating Web sites using its innovative visual tools."

Microsoft Press Release

In 1994, Charles Ferguson – consultant, writer and holder of a Ph.D. from the Massachusetts Institute of Technology – set up a company called Vermeer Technologies, named after his favourite painter. It was not the easiest of times to launch a startup in Silicon Valley, with the US emerging gingerly from a recession, a flat stock market, and the Internet yet to be taken seriously by those with money to invest. Yet within two years he sold the company to Microsoft for $133 million, in the process making a fortune for himself and his associates.

Vermeer's "very cool, very big idea" was FrontPage, the first software product for creating and managing a website, which is now bundled with Microsoft Office and boasts several million users worldwide.

Ferguson tells the story of Vermeer in his book *High Stakes, No Prisoners: a winner's tale of greed and glory in the internet wars* (Times

Business Books, 1999). But this is not just another self-congratulatory business book about how somebody made millions on the market. Ferguson gives a "warts and all" view into the inner workings of Silicon Valley. In one of his most memorable lines, he describes it as a place where "one finds little evidence that the meek shall inherit the earth."

Ferguson is unerringly candid throughout the book, naming names of the people he came across – many of them big movers and the shakers in the industry – and saying what he really thinks of them. Ferguson is very tough on himself, too, owning up to the mistakes his start-up made, and detailing his own shortcomings as a person and a businessman. There cannot be many business books around where the index lists, under the heading of the author's name, "mistakes of," "naïveté of," and "paranoia of."

This is how Ferguson describes a ten-week period beginning in early September of 1995, when Vermeer Technologies went from being an unknown development-phase company to being the hottest, coolest start-up in the United States:

"September through Christmas 1995 would prove to be the most exciting yet punishing months of my professional life.

"One year earlier, we'd had to fight for months to raise $4 million. Even in March, when we had tried to counter NaviSoft's product launch, nobody had paid us the slightest attention. But by the end of September, we had the opposite problem, and it was a very serious problem indeed. Everyone either wanted a piece of our hide or they wanted us dead because we threatened them. And my problems were by no means confined to the outside world. To the contrary, I needed to defend both Vermeer and myself against our investors and our newly-hired CEO just as much as against external threats. Events were moving at the speed of light, everything was connected to everything else, and there was essentially nobody I could talk to about it. So these developments brought astonishing highs and great personal fulfilment, but also brutal fights, extreme stress, and painful lessons.

"Even through August, we had been quite secretive. While we had been speaking to potential partners, large customers, and analysts, we did so very selectively, under nondisclosure, and usually without revealing sensitive technology or strategic plans. But by September our product was nearly done, and it was time to announce ourselves to the world. Our timing was perfect; as we had planned, we could launch in the peak of the fall season. We wanted business, and there was no further point in concealing what either we or our product did. Furthermore, it was also time to raise more money. So it was time to show our stuff. When we did the response was, as they say, overwhelming.

"So when Peter Amstein and I arrived at the room we'd been assigned for our presentation at Dick Shaffer's Digital Media Outlook conference on September 11, 1995, we found the place packed and the atmosphere electric. Every seat and every square inch was occupied. Venture capitalists, investment bankers, technology executives, and industry gurus were lined up along the walls, with more straining to hear from the doorway and the corridor outside. Everyone had already heard of us, but none of them had ever seen our presentations or software before. They liked what they saw. Afterward we were surrounded by people shoving cards at us, wanting meetings, asking if we were raising money, inviting us to conferences, offering partnerships."

Analysis

The Vermeer start up and sale is an example of strategy in the fast lane. Remember that Charles Ferguson launched Vermeer Technologies from his original idea in late 1993, started shipping FrontPage 1.0 in October 1995, and had sold the company by Christmas of that year. Ferguson himself describes start-ups as "the intellectual equivalent of driving a small, fast convertible with the top down, the stereo playing Keith Jarrett, Bach, or J.J. Cale very loud, doing a hundred miles an hour on an empty road at sunset."

Strategy is not always about carefully considered actions and well thought-through plans. For Ferguson, the experience was visceral, immediate, and intense.

In terms of the strategic lessons that can be drawn from this example, we need to start by acknowledging that Ferguson achieved something pretty rare. For most of us, the chances of being acquired for massive dollars are about the same as the chances of winning the lottery. It could happen, but only a fool banks on it.

There are other, broader lessons. In general, companies that focus on acquisition put themselves in a dangerous position by closing off their options.

Also, there are relatively few potential suitors for most companies, and each may pass over a start-up for a variety of reasons – issues involving geography, personalities, or technical integration for example. Finally, it is worth remembering that a buyout is driven by fundamentals like the quality of a company's management team, execution, technology, and strategy. Imitating what another company has done is generally a poor path to take.

Perhaps what the Vermeer story demonstrates above all is that the new economy is actually the entrepreneurial economy. As the pace of change in global markets and technology has accelerated, entrepreneurs have seized the opportunities created by that change. This can be a hugely profitable exercise, but the business highway is littered with the burnt-out wrecks of failed ventures.

CODA

There are more questions than answers. More than anything else, strategy is concerned with explaining organizational success. You might like to apply your knowledge of strategy to this account of the top-selling country singer Garth Brooks:

GARTH BROOKS CASE STUDY

Ask most people outside the US who is the top selling solo artist in US history and you are most unlikely to get the answer Garth Brooks. With global sales approaching 100 million the rise of Garth Brooks has been staggering. In 1992 alone, he accounted for 9% of EMI Music's $5 billion global sales. In 1997 his dispute with his American label, Capitol Nashville, raised more than a few industry eyebrows. Rumors abounded that Garth had demanded the resignation of Scott Hendricks, president/CEO of the label, before he would agree to the release of his latest set, *Sevens*. Although any link between the events has been strenuously denied by all parties, Scott Hendricks resigned in November 1997 and *Sevens* emerged within the month. Just how, in the words of Brooks himself, does "a guy with grey, thinning hair, an eating problem and in his 30s" outsell the likes of Elvis Presley, Michael Jackson, and Elton John, his nearest contenders?

With the benefit of hindsight, it is easy to talk of how Garth Brooks has achieved a perfect match with his market place. His sales figures match the rising importance of country music in the US which now accounts for 20% of music sales, his faith in God matches the rising spirituality evident across the globe, and his energy, enthusiasm and infectious sense of fun filled the vacuum created by an increasingly sterile pop music industry in the 1980s. But none of this could be anticipated or planned in some mechanical way before the event. Indeed, there are certainly better singers and writers than Garth Brooks, definitely better-looking guys, and without doubt better musicians. A panel of industry experts assembled at the beginning of 1989 would not, and indeed could not, have anticipated the Garth Brooks phenomenon.

So where does that leave us in explaining Garth's success? Perhaps it has something to do with the sheer passion he has for his vocation, his sense of alignment with what he is here to do and the powerful intent that he had to make it happen. The rest, as they say, is history. Garth himself is a little more modest:

"If God came down here with a box that had the reason in [for my success], I'd like to find just two words. The Music. That would be neat. I just hope they wouldn't read: The Hat."
Source: "Strategy from the Heart", Bob Gorzynski (1999)

And finally, just three questions you might like to reflect on:

» Do you agree with the views expressed in the article?
» Could the success of Garth Brooks been anticipated through a conventional planning process?
» If you were an entertainment executive today how would you identify the next Garth Brooks?

The purpose of the Garth Brooks case study is to encourage the recognition that there are limits to our level of understanding of organizational success. If we cannot readily explain the success of an individual musician, we must show some sense of humility when we are dealing with the much more complex world of organizations.

Key Concepts and Thinkers

Strategy has its own language. Get to grips with the lexicon of strategy through the *Express Exec* strategy glossary in this chapter, which also covers:

» key concepts;
» key thinkers.

Like many other business subjects, the theory and practice of strategy has a language of its own. Here is a selective glossary of some of the key terms, key concepts and key thinkers associated with the subject.

Activity-based management

This looks at the efficiency and effectiveness of delivering products and services to customers by analyzing the primary business processes that enable key customer needs to be met. This customer perspective breaks down the traditional functional silos since business processes are, by and large, activities that are linked *across* functional boundaries.

Affiliate marketing

A form of marketing pioneered by the likes of Amazon and CDNow: anybody with a website can sign up with them as a sales affiliate and receive a commission (typically between 5% and 15%) for any sales that are channeled through the affiliate site.

Ansoff, Igor

Distinguished academic and consultant, who introduced a number of key ideas – including gap analysis, synergy, corporate advantage, and paralysis by analysis – which helped to form the basic vocabulary of modern-day strategic thinking. His first, and most influential, book *Corporate Strategy* was published in 1962.

Architecture

Term used by John Kay in his book *Foundations of Corporate Success* (1992) to describe a system of relationships within an organization, or between an organization and its employees, suppliers and customers, or all of them.

Balanced scorecard

Concept developed by Robert S. Kaplan and David P. Norton of the Harvard Business School, that supplements traditional financial performance measures with new measures based on customer, internal business process and innovation, and learning measures. However, the balanced scorecard goes beyond the use of key performance indicators because it specifically integrates accounting and financial information into a management system that focuses the entire organization on implementing its long-term strategy.

Bricks and mortar

Companies that use traditional methods of selling and distributing products.

Business strategy

Concerned with market positioning and segmentation, matching business structures, following through cost leadership, differentiation, and specialization strategies at SBU level.

Business process re-design

This involves changing both organizational structure and processes to ensure that future customer needs can be anticipated and fulfilled in the most cost-effective manner. It should not be confused with crude cost-cutting exercises (such as downsizing) although many organizations have used both approaches simultaneously, with the result that the value of process redesign has been permanently tarnished in the eyes of many managers.

Chandler, Alfred

Born in 1918, Chandler is a Pulitzer Prize-winning business historian who was very influential in shaping the way organizations thought about strategy in the 1960s and 1970s. He was the first person to make explicit the link between strategy and structure.

Choiceboards

Interactive, on-line systems that let people design their own products from a menu of attributes, prices, and delivery options.

Clusters

Critical masses of linked industries in one location which enjoy a high level of success in their particular field. Famous examples are

Silicon Valley and Hollywood, but clusters can be found everywhere. According to Michael Porter, clusters can affect competition in three ways:

» by increasing the productivity of companies based in the area;
» by driving the direction and speed of innovation in their field;
» by stimulating the formation of new businesses within the cluster.

Competitive advantage

John Kay, following in the footsteps of Michael Porter, defines competitive advantage as: "The application of distinctive capability to a specific market place differentiating an organization from its competitors and allowing it to achieve above-average returns in that market."

Competitive convergence

This is what happens when companies are drawn towards imitation and homogeneity. The result is often static or declining prices, and downward pressures on costs, which combine to compromize the ability of companies to invest in the business in the long term.

Competitive intelligence

In a world of rapid technological change where new and sometimes surprising competitors can suddenly appear, a company's success will increasingly depend on how effectively it can gather, analyze, and use information. According to Larry Kahaner, author of a book on the subject, companies that can turn raw information into powerful intelligence will "build market share, launch new products, increase profits, and destroy competitors."

Confusion marketing

A method used by some businesses to deny customers the means of making an informed choice through swamping them with an excess of confusing price information. The intention is clear – to make price comparisons with rivals impossible in practical terms. The hope is that customers will give up in frustration and stay with, or move to, well-known companies or brands. Customers signing up for a mobile phone or obtaining a mortgage for house purchase often find themselves facing confusion marketing tactics.

Core competencies

These are the key strengths of an organization (sometimes called distinctive capabilities). Gary Hamel and C.K. Prahalad, authors of *Competing for the Future*, define core competencies as "a bundle of skills and technologies (rather than a simple or discrete skill or technology) that enables the company to provide a particular benefit to customers."

Core competents

The small number of people in an organization who are absolutely vital to that organization's success. Bill Gates has reflected that if 20 people were to leave Microsoft, the company would risk bankruptcy. In a study by the Corporate Leadership Council, a computer firm recognized 100 core competents out of 16,000 employees; a software company had 10 out of 11,000; and a transportation group deemed 20 of its 33,000 as really critical.

Corporate strategy

Corporate strategy is concerned with mission and vision, portfolio management, acquisitions, and divestments. Generic corporate strategies include growth, portfolio extension, caretaking, harvesting, and retrenchment.

Cost leadership

When an organization sets out to become the lowest cost producer in its industry, it does this by exploiting *economies of scale* or *scope* (including marketing and promotional expenditure necessary to maintain reputation or brand image), and the *experience/learning curve* (over time experience results in better ways of doing things and this leads to lower costs). Cost leadership does *not* imply substandard goods or poor quality, it simply means delivering goods and services to customers at the quality level expected at the lowest price (as determined by the customer!).

Critical success factors

These are the key organizational capabilities that differentiate competitors in an industry by their ability to meet customer needs.

Cultural diagnostics

Cultural diagnosis is a vital part of the strategic process because it allows us to become aware of the filters that we use to process our experience, both as individuals and as members of organizations, and the degree of selectivity that is involved in interpreting those experiences. It is a complex area, not least because it deals directly with the individual foibles that we all have as human beings.

Customer intimacy

Building customer loyalty in the long term by continually tailoring and shaping products and services to the needs of an increasingly choosy customer. Organizations pursuing this strategy frequently try to build lifetime relationships with their customers.

Customer relationship management (CRM)

A set of techniques and approaches designed to provide personalized service to customers and to increase customer loyalty. Increasingly viewed as a strategic issue, it is one that typically requires technological support.

Customer sacrifice

The gap between what customers settle for and what they really want. Successful companies reduce customer sacrifice by cultivating learning relationships. The more customers "teach" the company, the better it can provide just what they want – and the more difficult it becomes for competitors, to whom customers would have to teach their preferences afresh, to lure them away.

Data mining

The process of using advanced statistical tools to identify commercially-useful patterns or relationships in databases.

Data warehouse

A database that can access all of a company's information.

Differentiation

The ability to be unique in an industry along some dimensions valued by the customer: for example, through product or service leadership, or through understanding and knowing customers better than competitors do.

Discontinuities

One-off changes in the market place that force radical organizational change.

Disintermediation

Buzzword for how the Internet is cutting out the middlemen, enabling wholesalers/manufacturers to sell direct to the end user. Classic potential victims of disintermediation are estate agents and travel agents.

Downsizing

Restructuring in a declining market where the level of resources (such as manpower, support functions and other factors) are inappropriate to meeting current customer needs.

e-business

Using the Internet or other electronic means to conduct business. The two most common models are B2C (business-to-consumer) and B2B (business-to-business). Partly due to news coverage given to high profile companies like Amazon, B2C is the better known model; on the other hand, B2B probably has more long-term potential than its more glamorous cousin.

e-commerce

Commercial activity conducted via the Internet.

e-tailing

Retail strategy based on selling and order processing via the web.

External positioning

The relationship between an organization and the external world, in terms of its markets, customers, and the broader environment.

External risks

Dangers posed by the outside world, predictable or unexpected. These might include possible reactions from competitors, media attacks, or threats to market demand from legislation or substitution.

Focus

A concept popularized by Michael Porter, focus involves selecting a market segment or group of segments within an industry, and serving customers in these segments to the exclusion of others.

Functional strategies

Tools for translating corporate/business strategies into concrete operational strategies.

Gap analysis

A method for exploring the gap between current reality and the vision of the organization, both in terms of external customer needs and internal capabilities.

Globalization

The integration of economic activity across national or regional boundaries; a process that is being accelerated by the impact of information technology.

Infomediary

A company or individual that makes money by bridging the gap between the need of companies to capture detailed customer information and the desire of customers for protection of such information from exploitation by companies.

Informate

Term coined by Harvard academic Shoshana Zuboff to describe the capacity for information technology to translate and make visible organizational processes, objects, behaviors, and events.

Innovation

A significant change or improvement in the products or services of an organization, or the process by which they are produced.

Intellectual capital

Intellectual capital is intellectual material – knowledge, information, intellectual property, experience – that can be put to use to create wealth. In a business context, intellectual capital is the total of what the employees in an organization know that gives it a competitive edge.

Internal capabilities or competencies

What the organization is good at. John Kay refers to distinctive capabilities as "something an organization can do that its potential competitors cannot . . . based on its unique set of relationships in the market place."

Internal constraints

These are factors that can inhibit an organization's ability to achieve desired outcomes. These factors include the level of resources available, knowledge of new markets and products, and the cultural adaptability of the organization to new opportunities.

Intranet

A network designed to organize and share information that is accessible only by a specified group or organization.

Key performance indicator (KPI)

Key performance indicators are normally combined as a basket of measures to cover all critical areas of an organization. Although the choice of specific indicators will depend on the unique circumstances of each organization, KPIs are generally selected from the following categories of information: customer satisfaction; product and service innovation; operational improvement; employee morale and commitment; financial health; and cultural diagnosis.

Killer app

A killer app ("app" is short for "application") is a new good or service that, by being first in the market place, dominates it, often returning several hundred percent on the initial investment.

Knowledge management

A system, most often computer-based, to share information in a company with the goal of increasing levels of responsiveness and innovation.

Mass customization

The cost-efficient mass production as a matter of routine of goods and services in lot sizes of one, or just a few at a time.

Mintzberg, Henry

A member of McGill University's Faculty of Management since 1968, Mintzberg has written extensively about the process of strategy formation, and the design of organizations. His best-known books include *The Nature of Managerial Work* (1973), *The Structuring of Organizations* (1979), *Power In and Around Organizations* (1983), *The Strategy Process* (1988, 2nd edn 1991), and *Mintzberg on Management: Inside Our Strange World of Organizations* (1989). His book *The Rise and Fall of Strategic Planning* won the best book award of the Academy of Management in 1995.

Mission

Many organizations have acknowledged the importance of purpose by framing a formal mission statement. In theory, a mission statement should capture the essence of an organization and those things about it which are truly unique, and should provide the platform from which the organization can create the future. Management writers sometimes refer to this as establishing purpose or strategic intent. The statement takes the form of a formal declaration of what an organization is all about, rooted in a clear understanding of reality. In practical terms, mission statements rarely live up to very much and are often little more than a collection of management buzzwords that are not rooted in organizational reality.

New capitalism

According to Robert Reich, former US Secretary for Labor, "Old capitalism's giant companies had vast numbers of employees; new capitalism's giant companies have few employees. The issues of old capitalism – law on property, contract, limited liability, tort, bankruptcy – all of these are no longer really appropriate. The key assets of new capitalism are not defined as physical property but as intellectual assets, many embedded in people."

One-to-one marketing

Customizing and personalizing a product or service to meet an individual customer's specific needs.

Operational excellence

Providing customers with reliable products or services at competitive prices and delivered with minimal difficulty or inconvenience. The object of the organization adopting this strategy is to lead its industry in price and convenience.

Pascale, Richard

Born in 1938, Richard Pascale was a member of the faculty of Stanford's Graduate School of Business for 20 years. Now a leading business consultant, he has written or co-authored three highly challenging books – *The Art of Japanese Management* (1981), *Managing on the Edge* (1990), and *Surfing on the Edge of Chaos* (2000).

Porter, Michael

Born in 1947 and now a Harvard Business School professor, Porter is perhaps the best known name in the field of business strategy, and the person who has done most to turn strategy into a scholarly discipline. His "Five forces" model, described in this book, sometimes called the 'Porter model' (see below), is a cornerstone of MBA program world-wide. He has published many books and articles, the best known being *Competitive Strategy* (1980) and *Competitive Advantage* (1985). Much of Porter's thinking appears first in the pages of the Harvard Business Review.

Porter model

This model states that the profitability of an industry is determined by five basic competitive forces:

» Bargaining power of buyers relative to firms in the industry.
» Bargaining power of suppliers relative to firms in the industry.
» Ease of entry of new firms into the industry.
» Availability of substitute products.
» Intensity of rivalry between existing firms in the industry.

Product leadership

An organization achieves this by creating a continuous stream of state of the art products and services.

Product overlap

This occurs when more than one generation of the same product is available simultaneously. The original version of a piece of software may sell at a reduced price alongside the latest version which commands a higher price.

Prospect theory

According to prospect theory, people are more motivated by their losses than their gains, and this results in increasingly risky behavior as losses accumulate. For example, long-odds bets are more popular in the last horse-race of the day than in the first. By the end of the day, punters have lost most of their gambling money and hope to win it all back with a single long-shot bet that they would not have considered taking on the first race, when they believe that they have everything to play for.

Push technology

The delivery of news and multimedia information via the World Wide Web to personal computers on people's desks. The web is basically a "pull" medium. Users decide what they want, point their browsers at the relevant website and then pull the designated pages back to their PCs.

Reality check

A reality check is any tool, technique, method or device used by both individuals and organizations to provide feedback on their place in the world. Reality checks include tools and techniques that are recognized as strategic (such as industry analysis, competitor analysis and other devices) and many others that are not (customer research, employee feedback, or merely reading trade magazines). In fact, any exercise which might increase organizational awareness is an important part of the strategic process whether it has a strategic label or not.

Re-purposing

Originally coined by US TV executives to describe the process of "freshening-up" a new series of a well-established TV show, whose popularity is flagging, by introducing new characters and plot-lines. The term is now being adopted by companies seeking to re-establish forward momentum.

Scenario fixations

This is believing that one thing is happening when the reality is completely different. It can happen to groups as well as to individuals. In 1988, the warship USS *Vincennes* was involved with potentially hostile Iranian vessels. A series of rapid maneuvers added to the tension and, in the general confusion, the crew incorrectly identified a civilian Airbus 320 as an Iranian F14 fighter, then misheard its identification signals, and mistakenly thought that it was descending towards the ship when it was in fact on its usual flight-path. The warship fired two missiles at the airliner, killing all 290 passengers. The ship's computer system had performed perfectly throughout.

Scenario planning

A tool pioneered by Shell in the 1970s that involves identifying and planning for a range of possible futures. The idea, in a nutshell, is to improve a company's capacity to respond to whichever future comes to pass.

Seven-S model

A widely-used analytical tool, devised by Richard Pascale and Anthony Athos, that evaluates organizations under seven key headings to which managers need to pay particular attention. The seven are: Strategy; Structure; Systems; Skills; Style; Shared values; and Staff. Some of these areas are "hard" (i.e. strategy, structure, and systems), and some are "soft" (style, staff, and shared values). "Skills" is placed centrally because it is both "hard" and "soft", comprising both the distinctive capabilities of key personnel and the core competencies of the organization as a whole.

Shared vision

In a corporation, a shared vision changes people's relationship with the company. It is no longer "their company", it becomes "*our* company." A shared vision is the first step in allowing people who mistrusted each other to begin to work together. It creates a common identity.

Strategic architecture

A term first used by Gary Hamel and C.K. Prahalad to refer to an organization's high-level blueprint for developing the new competencies and capabilities that it needs to achieve its vision for the future. As such, it emphasizes the importance of the multitude of individual networks and linkages that underlie successful change.

Strategic assets

Market position (for example, a monopolistic or oligopolistic position), or relationship with a nation state or regional economic bloc.

Strategic drift

The financial performance of an organization reflects its key strengths and weaknesses in the past. Incremental changes in key markets may go unnoticed because sales and profits lag behind changes in the reality of the market place. The organization may experience its margins and profits being squeezed yet take comfort in the fact that sales continue to hold up or even rise. If the organization fails to tackle the root cause of its problems at customer level, sales will begin to decline, and profits may fall precipitously. Strategic drift is often caused when discontinuities go unnoticed because there is a significant time lag before they hit financial performance.

Strategic inflection point

A term coined by Andy Grove to describe a moment in the life of a business when its fundamentals are about to change for better or worse.

Strategic positioning

How an organization can achieve market distinction by performing different activities from those of its rivals, or by performing similar activities in different ways.

Technology adoption life cycle

A model created by Geoffrey A. Moore to demonstrate the various points at which individuals will become involved with a technological innovation. Moore identified five key groups which will become involved with any new technology at various stages of its life cycle:

» *Innovators*: the technology enthusiasts
» *Early adopters*: the visionaries
» *Early majority*: the pragmatists
» *Late majority*: the conservatives
» *Laggards*: the sceptics

Trade-offs

A company must sometimes abandon or forego some product features, services, or activities in order to be unique at others. Such trade-offs, in the product and in the value chain, are what make a company truly distinctive. When improvements in the product or in the value chain do not require trade-offs, they often become new best practices which are imitated because competitors can do so with no sacrifice to their existing ways of competing.

Ten-X force

A term used by Andy Grove in his book *Only the Paranoid Survive*. It describes a super-competitive force that threatens the future of a business.

Unique selling proposition (USP)

Best defined as a company's unique point of difference, the USP of an organization is the unique way in which it matches its internal capabilities with external market opportunities in order to gain competitive advantage.

Value added

In essence, value added is the difference between the value of a firm's output and the cost of the firm's inputs. Technically, it is the difference between the market value of output and the cost of inputs including the cost of capital. (It is the latter which differentiates a value-added statement from a profit or loss statement.) It can also be expressed as a ratio (value added as a proportion of a firm's net or gross output). In practice, however, measurement of value added is difficult because of the many invisible/psychological attributes of products or services.

Value proposition

A set of benefits that a company can offer its customers which are different from those that competitors offer.

Viral marketing

Releasing a catchy message, typically using on-line technology, with a view to the message reaching growing numbers of people, initially organically but then exponentially.

Vision

A company's view of its future that is compelling and stretching, but also viewed as achievable. A corporate vision for the future has to be grounded in awareness. If it is not, it quickly becomes a wish-driven strategy – meritorious in all respects except for the fact that it will never be achieved.

Resources

Countless words have been written about strategy. This chapter identifies the best resources:

» books and articles on strategy;
» articles;
» journals, magazines and websites.

ANNOTATED BIBLIOGRAPHY

Over the years, literally thousands of books have been published about strategy. Here is a list of some of the best:

Aldrich, D.F. (2000) *Mastering The Digital Marketplace: Practical Strategies For Competitiveness In The New Economy*, **John Wiley, New York**

In the digital economy, argues Aldrich, there are two key measures of value: time (as in how much time your product or service will save the customer) and content (information, knowledge, or services that provide added value to the customer). He goes on to outline a new business model which he calls the Digital Value Network (DVN), a community of electronically-linked business partners who work together to produce value for the customer as the customer defines it, and offers strategies for creating and sustaining it.

Burton-Jones A. (1999) *Knowledge Capitalism*, **Oxford University Press, Oxford**

Burton-Jones marshals an impressive range of evidence in this closely-argued exploration of how the shift to a knowledge-based economy is redefining the shape and nature of organizations. He also describes the emergence of a new breed of capitalist, one dependent on knowledge rather than physical resources. There are plenty of easier reads about the knowledge economy on the market, but those looking for substance rather than eye-catching glibness will be pleased to find in *Knowledge Capitalism* a book that provides frequent moments of insight without ever compromising gravitas.

Campbell A. & Goold M. (1998) *Synergy*, **Capstone, Oxford**

Subtitled *Why links between business units often fail and how to make them work*, this is an insightful and penetrating guide to how and under what circumstances a business portfolio can be worth more than the sum of its parts. Campbell and Goold describe synergy as "the strategist's holy grail." If you can get the disparate elements of an organization to work together, the authors maintain, there is an opportunity to create more value without using more resources. They go on to explain why synergy can sometimes be difficult to achieve, how to assess the potential benefits, when and how parent companies should intervene to create synergy, the pros and cons of synergy, and how to evaluate the success of synergy interventions.

Creelman J. (1998) *Building and Implementing a Balanced Scorecard*, Business Intelligence, London

It is now around five years since Robert Kaplan and David Norton first wrote about the Balanced Scorecard in a Harvard Business Review article. For anybody unfamiliar with the concept, the Balanced Scorecard translates an organization's mission and strategy into a comprehensive set of performance measures that provides the framework for a strategic measurement and management system. While the Scorecard's originators have produced a number of books and articles developing and extending the concept, they have been less convincing on some of the practical challenges and issues involved in implementing a Scorecard within an organization. This informative and highly readable report fills that gap admirably, containing as it does instructive case studies, informed and clear-eyed commentary on the benefits and difficulties associated with putting a Scorecard in place, and regular summaries. The report is not cheap but any company planning to build and implement its own Scorecard would soon recoup the outlay on this report through time saved and mistakes avoided.

de Geus A. (1997) *The Living Company*, Nicholas Brealey, London

Drawing on unpublished research conducted by Shell in the early 1980s, Arie de Geus – the man widely credited for originating the concept of the "learning organization" – believes that most companies fail because they focus too narrowly on financial performance and pay insufficient attention to themselves as communities of human beings with the potential to learn, adapt and grow. The living company, he says, emphasizes knowledge rather than capital, and adaptability rather than core competencies. De Geus won the Edwin G. Booz prize for Most Insightful Management Book back in 1997 and so it is a little disappointing that his ideas have not yet broken through into the mainstream. Even so, anybody with an interest in organizational learning will find something of value here.

Drucker P. (1993) *Post-Capitalistic Society*, HarperCollins, New York

An early picture of the new economy which has held up extremely well over the intervening years. Tom Peters may be the most famous living management guru, but Peter Drucker is probably the most respected and insightful.

Easton J. (1999) *StrikingitRich.com*, McGraw-Hill, New York

Sub-titled *Profiles of 23 incredibly successful companies you've probably never heard of*, Jaclyn Easton's rigorously researched and extremely readable book proves that websites do not have to be high profile extravaganzas to make serious money. The sites which she discusses demonstrate that it is perfectly possible for a website to achieve a profit quickly if an idea is well-conceived and executed and if start-up costs are managed tightly.

Evans P. & Wurster T. (2000) *Blown to Bits*, Harvard Business School Press, Boston

Those of us in the business of communicating information to others have until now faced a strategic choice, which can be characterized as richness or reach. Providing rich, customized information about a product or service necessarily limited the number of potential customers that could be reached with that information. On the other hand, going for reach necessarily meant the degree of customization of the information reduced in direct correlation with the widening universe of customers. So, which to go for? According to Evans and Wurster, two consultants from the Boston Consulting Group, this dilemma is fast disappearing as advanced digital technologies are allowing information to separate from its physical carrier. This, in effect, kills off the richness/reach trade-off and renders many traditional business structures, and the strategies that drive them, obsolete.

Ghoshal S. & Bartlett C.A. (1998) *The Individualized Corporation*, Heinemann, London

In a series of landmark articles in the Harvard Business Review, the authors developed a new framework for the strategic process which is based on purpose, processes and people rather than the more familiar model of strategy, structure and systems . *The Individualized Corporation* takes this work further, revealing the emergence of a fundamentally different management philosophy that focuses on the power of the individual as the driver of value creation. The book is an insightful and stimulating read which has culminated from six years of research and hundreds of interviews with managers in companies such as Intel, ABB, Canon and 3M.

Gladwell M. (2000) *The Tipping Point: how little things can make a big difference*, Little, Brown, London

Why do some minority tastes remain strictly minority, while others extend into the mainstream? *The Tipping Point* is a well-written and racy exploration of what lies behind the point when a small fad acquires critical mass and takes off. It's very readable but the central idea isn't really enough to sustain a whole book – no surprise then to discover that it began its life as a long article in *New Yorker* magazine.

Heller R. (1997) *In Search of European Excellence*, HarperCollins Business, London

With a nod to the Peters and Waterman classic, Heller sets out to identify the key strategies with which Europe's most successful companies are beating their competition. When he looked at the state of European business, he found that Europe's old reactionaries are still in the majority, but that their ascendancy is rapidly draining away as new leaders act decisively in ten arenas of corporate renaissance. These include devolving leadership, driving radical change, reshaping culture, keeping the competitive edge, and achieving total management quality. In each area, Heller gives convincing examples of European companies that have made wholehearted efforts to change. As ever with a book that draws on a large number of case studies, one or two of the companies praised have slipped from grace in recent times. This does not undermine Heller's basic thesis, but it does demonstrate how tough it is to hold onto industry leadership once it has been attained.

Hobsbawm E. (2000) *The New Century*, Little, Brown, London

In this book, the pre-eminent historian (you will not find a better account of the twentieth century than his *Age of Extremes*) offers his analysis of the current state of the world. Although the scope of this book goes much wider than the new economy, there is one chapter in particular – called *The global village* – that offers a lucid, cool-headed, and reasoned assessment of the global economy. This is a much-needed antidote to the starry-eyed hyperbole that seems to dominate the globalization debate.

Hutton W. & Giddens A. (2000) *On the Edge*, Jonathan Cape, London

On the Edge draws together ten original contributions by leading thinkers like Paul Volcker, Manuel Castells, Arlie Russell Hochschild and George Soros. The overall conclusion seems to be that global capitalism does have huge potential for good but is just as likely to create a set of consequences that most of us would rather avoid. Co-author and Industrial Society boss Will Hutton describes global capitalism as "precarious and potentially dangerous." An important book that takes a clear-eyed view of its subject.

Kaplan R.S. & Norton D.P. (1996) *The Balanced Scorecard*, Harvard Business School, Boston

Many management writers have written in general terms on the limitations of relying on traditional financial measures to assess business performance. But few have set out specifically with the aim of building a comprehensive framework of broadly-based performance measures that provides a process for organizations to link long-term strategic objectives with short-term actions. By doing precisely this, Kaplan and Norton have taken performance measurement to the heart of organizational success in the long term. The authors demonstrate how to use measures in four categories – financial performance, customer knowledge, internal business processes, and learning and growth – to build a robust learning system that aligns individual, organizational, and cross-departmental initiatives in building long-term strategic advantage.

Kelly S. & Allison M.A. (1999) *The Complexity Advantage*, McGraw-Hill, New York

This book argues that anybody operating in a business world growing ever more complex would benefit from an understanding of complexity theory. *The Complexity Advantage* represents a serious and sustained attempt to incorporate complexity principles and methodologies into business thinking. The more general reader may initially be baffled by some of the terminology but persistence will pay off.

Law A. (1998) *Open Minds*, Orion, London

St Luke's is a high-profile London-based advertising agency and Andy Law has been the company's iconoclastic chairman since 1995. The company is owned entirely by its employees, and all physical resources – offices, PCs etc. – in the company are shared: there is little hierarchy. Employees are involved in almost all decisions, including setting their own pay rises. Whether the model developed at St Luke's has the resilience to cope with a down-turn in its business fortunes (the company has enjoyed continuous growth since its creation) remains to be seen. In the meantime, *Open Minds* makes a compelling case study, describing and explaining as it does the business practices and philosophy behind this fascinating company.

Lewis J. (1999) *Trusted Partners*, Free Press, New York

Mergers and alliances on an ever-grander scale are a feature of the global economy. *Trusted Partners* describes how to build trust between organizations that are forging alliances of various types with other companies, and explores how interpersonal relationships are a critical element of that. Drawing on experience built over four decades of working with some of the world's leading companies, Lewis goes well beyond theoretical analysis of the nature of trust between corporate rivals to lay out some practical and eminently sensible steps involved in building and maintaining trust.

Moore J.F. (1996) *The Death of Competition*, Wiley, New York

Business as ecosystem – Moore explores the biological metaphor in great detail and with considerable insight. One of the first explorations, and arguably the best, of leadership and strategy in a future which Moore envisions will be characterized by organized chaos.

Porter M. (1980) *Competitive Strategy*, Free Press, New York

What forces drive competition in an industry? How can a company be best placed to compete in the long run? Porter's book, radical in its day, was one of the first to look the whole field of competitive strategy. His work has entered the management mainstream, and his techniques for analyzing industries and competitors are now widely used. For anybody wishing to increase their awareness of the industry or competitive context that they work in, Porter's models and techniques remain valid and easy to use.

Read T., Chace C. & Rowe S. (2000) *The Internet Start-Up Bible*, Random House, New York

The Internet Start-Up Bible is an accessible, well-written guide about how to plan, research, fund, market and implement a successful Internet-based business model. The authors take the logical and too-often neglected step of applying the same success criteria to dot-com business start-ups as to traditional ventures. Detailed chapters on business planning and on attracting venture capital are followed by sections on various aspects of starting up an Internet business; technology, design, marketing, and launch, before concluding with business growth and flotation. The book is crammed with useful case studies, extensive links and contact addresses, and running quotes from business gurus and key books.

Ringland G. (1988) *Scenario Planning*, Wiley, Chichester

Gill Ringland, ICL's group executive with responsibility for strategy, adds her contribution to the plethora of books published about scenario planning. It gives a nuts-and-bolts account of ICL's experience of building scenarios, as well as drawing on examples from companies

like British Airways and United Distillers. It should appeal to its target
audience of managers who have not come across the idea in any detail
before.

Schwartz E. (1999) *Digital Darwinism*, Penguin, New York

A book title that brings together two of the biggest managerial
buzzwords of recent times exerts a certain fascination. According
to Schwartz in an interview published on Amazon.com, *Digital Darwinism* is "a different way of looking at the Web economy and how
it's co-evolving with the larger business world around it. It's a way of
looking at the Web as an ecosystem, where the players are scrounging
for money and are competing and co-operating with each other as if
they were a species in a natural environment." This is a fascinating
premise and one which merits rather more depth than Schwartz brings
to the topic. There is a 17-page introduction entitled "Frenetic Evolution" in which he notes some interesting parallels between Darwin's
theory of evolution and the on-line world. But he goes no further
in substantive terms. There are a few links made to what lies at the
heart of Digital Darwinism, namely "seven breakthrough strategies for
surviving in the cut-throat Web economy," but occasional allusions
to "survival guides" don't constitute the grand theory that Schwartz
seems to promise at the outset. The irony is that the seven strategies
themselves are a neat encapsulation of what a business – whether an
Internet start-up or a bricks-and-mortar offshoot – should be doing to
achieve Web success.

Senge P. (1990) *The Fifth Discipline*, Doubleday, New York

Peter Senge's book was one of the first to popularize the concept of
the learning organization. His five core disciplines that underpin the
building of a learning community are Personal Mastery, Mental Models
(the filters through which we view the world), Shared Vision, Team
Learning and Systems Thinking. The last of these, which Senge terms
the cornerstone discipline, is covered in 70 pages in a section that
represents an excellent generalist introduction to the main concepts of
systems thinking, a core skill in a globalized, networked economy.

Slywotzky A.J., Morrison D.J., Moser T., Mundt K.A. & Quella J.A. (1999) *Profit Patterns*, John Wiley, New York

A total re-questioning of different types of profit models is a necessary aspect of success in the new economy. In *Profit Patterns*, the authors introduce pattern thinking as a means of enabling managers to envision opportunities and design winning strategies ahead of the competition. "Like the best chess players," they write, "masters of business pattern recognition, instead of seeing chaos, know how to identify the strategic picture unfolding within the complexity and discover the pattern behind it all." The book describes a set of 30 patterns that have occurred in industry after industry, shifting billions of pounds in market value from those who "missed" them to those who "mastered" them. Company case studies featured in the book include Dell, Microsoft and Amazon. Not a particularly easy read, but one that rewards attention.

Stewart T.A. (1997) *Intellectual Capital: the New Wealth of Organizations*, Nicholas Brealey, Naperville

This book has proved itself in the market place as the definitive guide to understanding and managing intangible assets. The author provides a framework, practical guide, and theory of the significance of intellectual capital (defined by Stewart as "packaged useful knowledge") which is a delight to read. In an age of lightweight books on the new information age, this book is a heavyweight which explains why intellectual capital will be the foundation of corporate success in the new century.

Van der Heijden K. (1996) *Scenarios: the Art of Strategic Conversation*, Wiley, Chichester

Van der Heijden, a former head of Shell's Business Environment Division, takes as his startpoint a belief that uncertainty "has the effect of moving the key to success from the optimal strategy to the most skilful strategic process." After setting out the principles of scenario planning, he moves onto a highly practical section discussing how to help a management team broaden its views and think more strategically about the future.

Wriston W. (1992) *Twilight of Sovereignty*, **Charles Scribner's Sons, New York**

Walt Wriston, former chairman of Citicorp, addresses the issues facing the corporations of America and the world during the 1990s and beyond. He argues that centralized corporate/political power has disappeared, that the world has been transformed by technology, and that negotiation will rule the world in future.

ARTICLES (MOST RECENT FIRST)

"Can C.K. Prahalad Pass the Test?" *Fast Company* (August 2001). Can C.K. build a company around the principles that he has been teaching other high-powered leaders?

"A scary Swiss meltdown." *The Economist* (July 21, 2001). How a dud strategy brought a solid company to the brink of bankruptcy.

Willcocks L.P. & Plant R. (Spring 2001) "Pathways to e-business leadership: getting from bricks to clicks." *Sloan Management Review*.

"Change is sweet." *Fast Company* (June 2001). When is a Net strategy more than just a Net strategy?

"Over the counter e-commerce." *The Economist* (May 26, 2001).

"While Welch waited." *The Economist* (May 19, 2001). First in a series of case studies of how big established companies are developing their e-business strategies.

Porter M. (March 2001) "Strategy and the Internet." *Harvard Business Review*.

"Strategy Rule." *Fast Company* (January 2001).

"The rise of the infomediary." *The Economist* (June 26, 1999). The Internet is producing a string of racy new business models.

"A price on the priceless." *The Economist* (June 26, 1999). Companies know that their competitive advantage lies increasingly in knowledge and ideas. But what are the ideas worth?

Lovins A.B., Lovins L.H. & Hawken P. "A road map for natural capitalism." *Harvard Business Review* (May–June 1999).

Hagel J. & Singer M. "Unbundling the corporation." *Harvard Business Review* (March–April 1999).

"Internet economics." *The Economist* (December 12, 1998). Some companies succeed in the network economy, others do not. Why?

Nicholson N. "How hardwired is human behavior?" *Harvard Business Review* (July–August 1998).

Pine B.J. & Gilmore J.H. "Welcome to the experience economy." *Harvard Business Review* (July–August 1998).

"Business strategy: past, present and future." *The Economist* (July 11, 1998).

"Making strategy." *The Economist* (March 1, 1997).

Porter M. "What is strategy?" *Harvard Business Review* (November–December 1996).

Collins J.C. & Porras J.I. "Building your company's vision." *Harvard Business Review* (September–October 1996).

Bartlett C.A. & Ghoshal S. "Changing the role of top management: beyond systems to people." *Harvard Business Review* (May–June 1995).

Kotter J.P. "Leading change: why transformation efforts fail." *Harvard Business Review* (March–April 1995).

Bartlett C.A. & Ghoshal S. "Changing the role of top management: beyond structure to processes." *Harvard Business Review* (January–February 1995).

Bartlett C.A. & Ghoshal S. "Changing the role of top management: beyond strategy to purpose." *Harvard Business Review* (November–December 1994).

"The Vision Thing." *The Economist* (September 1994).

Mintzberg H. "The fall and rise of strategic planning." *Harvard Business Review* (January-February 1994).

"Business as war." *Fast Company* (November 1993). Business in the new economy is a civilized version of war. Companies, not countries, are battlefield rivals.

Kaplan R.S. & Norton D.P. "Putting the balanced scorecard to work." *Harvard Business Review* (September–October 1993).

Treacy M. & Wiersema F. "Customer intimacy and other value disciplines." *Harvard Business Review* (January–February 1993).

Stayer R. "How I learned to let my workers lead." *Harvard Business Review* (November–December 1990).

Mintzberg H. "Crafting strategy." *Harvard Business Review* (July–August 1987).

JOURNALS, MAGAZINES AND WEBSITES

For readers wanting to keep up to date with developments in the strategy field, the following publications and websites are worth dipping into on a regular basis:

Business Intelligence

Publishes some solid but very expensive reports (typically around £600 a copy). The website, however, carries some useful free material.
www.business-intelligence.co.uk/

Centre for Business Innovation

Site managed by consultants Ernst and Young – quality of content varies but occasionally provokes thought.
www.businessinnovation.ey.com

The Economist

The best single source of information about what is happening in the world. A mainstream publication but one that will take on some big topics from time to time, and one whose take on the new economy is variably insightful and clear-eyed.
www.economist.com

Fast Company

This monthly magazine has been an essential read since it started up in 1996. Of late, though, the content – whilst still excellent – has been swamped by increasing volumes of advertising. The companion website is just about the best free site around on the future world of work (it also carries material not found in the magazine).
www.fastcompany.com/home.html

Financial Times

Of all the dailies, *The Financial Times* provides the best in-depth coverage of strategy-related issues. Well worth keeping an eye out for their occasional Information Technology surveys as well as their monthly e-business magazine *Connectis*.

www.ft.com
www.ft.com/connectis

Harvard Business Review

The most authoritative business monthly on the block. Has tended in the past to be more mainstream than truly ground-breaking in its coverage of business issues. That said, HBR has responded well to the challenge to traditional business thinking posed by the new economy, and recent issues have generally contained two or three relevant articles. Also, if you are interested in getting the lowdown on forthcoming books from Harvard's publishing wing several months before publication, the magazine consistently trails major books with articles from the authors. The website provides an overview of the contents of the magazine – no free articles but the executive summaries are there and they are often all you need.
www.hbsp.harvard.edu/home.html

Internet Business

Just about the best of the recent flurry of new monthlies about doing business on the Internet. An informative mix of case studies, interviews, book extracts, and topical news stories.

Journal of Business Strategies

http://COBA.SHSU.edu/jbs/

New Scientist

Important science and technology stories will often appear here first. *New Scientist* also gives good coverage to emerging thinking in the scientific community.
www.newscientist.com

Red Herring

A monthly magazine that looks at the companies and trends that are shaping the business of technology. Occasionally prone to obsess about the technology itself rather than the impact of the technology.
www.redherring.com

Strategy & Business

An authoritative quarterly journal.
www.strategy-business.com/

Think Tanks

A good startpoint for exploring all the UK's major think tanks.
www.demos.co.uk/linkuk.htm

Wired magazine

A monthly American magazine that is good at picking up trends about
six months before they become trends.
www.wired.com/wired/

Ten Steps to Making Strategy Work

- » **Know where you're going and why**
  - » Develop a compelling vision
  - » The magic of intent
- » **Know where you are**
- » Develop awareness
- » Know your customers
- » **Choose your path**
  - » Evaluation and selection of strategic options
  - » Creativity
- » **Take Action**
  - » Leadership
  - » Trust
  - » Make it happen
- » **Monitor and adjust if necessary**
  - » Measure your performance

"Accidents and inspiration lead you to your destination."
From the song "The Long Way Home" by Mary Chapin
Carpenter

Life, as we know, is rarely neat. With the array of published materials on making and implementing strategic choices that have come from the likes of Chandler, Ansoff, Mintzberg, Porter, Pascale and others, plus a wealth of best-practice examples from companies world-wide, the strategy choice-board has never been so overwhelming.

Luke Rhinehart, in his book *The Dice Man*, described a character who made life decisions purely based on the random outcome of a throw of the dice. Whilst it may be true that any direction will do for a company that does not know where it wants to get to, it seems clear that a company with a well thought-through, coherent, focused strategy, born of a realistic appraisal of its own capabilities, is likely to outperform a competitor which has not been through that process.

There are no guarantees, of course. There is no inherent and absolute link between having good quality strategic processes in place and achieving a good business outcome. Sometimes companies undeservedly get lucky, sometimes good, well-founded decisions yield poor outcomes.

Most of us would accept that strategy has its place in modern organizational life. But which strategy? By now, it should be pretty apparent to the reader that there is no single best way for organizations and the people in them to think and act strategically.

The following ten points do not attempt to represent absolutely the strategic priorities for your organization right now. Some of the points may be irrelevant to your organization and its market place; there may be other points not covered. These points are best regarded as a set of generalized principles that will serve most organizations well most of the time.

The ten points can be summarized under five broad headings:

» Know where you are going and why
» Know where you are
» Choose your path

» Take action
» Monitor and adjust if necessary.

And these are the ten points:

Know where you are going and why
» Develop a compelling vision
» The magic of intent

Know where you are
» Develop awareness
» Know your customers

Choose your path
» Evaluation and selection of strategic options
» Creativity

Take Action
» Leadership
» Trust
» Make it happen

Monitor and adjust if necessary
» Measure your performance

1. DEVELOP A COMPELLING VISION

While not all writers believe that vision is the most appropriate term for the capacity to imagine and create the future (Gary Hamel and C.K. Prahalad talk in terms of *strategic intent* based on *foresight*), many recognize that successful organizations have a shared view of the future that stretches the organization beyond its current capabilities. Organizations which have fostered genuinely shared visions can, and do, create their futures, sometimes against overwhelming odds, by mobilizing the resources and commitment of their most valued assets, the people within them. Shared vision provides the emotional and intellectual energy for the strategic journey to bridge the gap between what is and what could be. Peter Senge, director of the Centre for Organizational Learning at MIT's Sloan School of Management, summarizes the position as follows:

> "At the heart of building shared vision is the task of designing and evolving ongoing processes in which people at every level of the organization, in every role, can speak from the heart about what really matters to them and be heard".
>
> *"The Fifth Discipline", Century Business, 1990*

Vision is deeply paradoxical. It is partly mystical, partly common sense. It is sometimes a picture of the future, sometimes a feeling. It is sometimes fully-formed, often not. But it is almost always the ability to see things differently or to integrate disparate and seemingly unrelated information in new ways. Sometimes it is merely asking questions that others cannot or will not ask. As John F. Kennedy put it: *"Some people see things and ask 'why', I see things and ask 'why not?'"*

Vision often has a strange magical quality to it; the ability to make the apparently impossible come true. As with Lee Teng-hui, president of Taiwan, it is sometimes the refusal to say "no":

> "Some say that it is impossible for us to break out of the diplomatic isolation we face, but we will do our utmost to demand the impossible."
>
> *Reported in "Time" magazine, June 19, 1995*

Some organizations (such as Sun Microsystems, Intuit, Monsanto and Amazon.com) talk in terms of visionary leaps into the future. Others plan their way into the future using much more pragmatic tools and techniques, which essentially extrapolate from the current situation. Different perspectives seem to suit different organizations, but they all share the same essential belief – namely that there is an identifiable future out there that is worth striving for.

2. THE MAGIC OF INTENT

Some organizations seem blessed with fortuitous circumstances, a strong sense of vision or purpose, good people, and a dynamic *can do* culture. These self-reinforcing characteristics allow these organizations to build on success, learn from failure, and sometimes literally re-invent themselves. At various stages of their corporate history, General Electric, 3M, and British Airways have all been textbook examples.

Meanwhile, most organizations seem to stumble along; content to be market followers in good times, desperate to defend themselves in bad times, sometimes to the point of survival itself. What distinguishes these two classes of organization? One answer is that it is the level of passion which infuses the organization in everything that it does. It is the power of intent or, more simply put, it is attitude. In the words of Goethe:

> "Whatever you can do, or dream you can, begin it.
> Boldness has genius and power and magic in it."

When we think of magic, we think of it in the context of the unusual, of make-believe kingdoms and Disney movies. Yet magic is all around us, both in our personal worlds and *especially* in our organizations and communities. Magic is simply the ability that all of us have to manifest what we truly are; the process of aligning ourselves to our deeper vision by following our passion.

Walk into some organizations and you feel this magic; it is tangible in the sense of aliveness, vitality, dynamism, and purpose that exists. On the other hand, we all know of organizations which stifle their members, where there is no sense of higher purpose, excitement or exhilaration with life. In the extreme, this can translate into a feeling that the war is long since lost even though the final battle has yet to be fought. Indeed, people working for such organizations often see the "end" as an almost desirable outcome, a release from the soul-destroying nature of their doomed organization.

Even so, organizations *can* be brought back from the brink of disaster, as the success stories of Chrysler and IBM illustrate. But to do so requires a fundamental shift in perspective; a recognition that strategy is much more than a bunch of tools and techniques.

3. DEVELOP AWARENESS

Awareness is the most important part of the strategic change cycle. For organizations, it starts with a close look at purpose (the corporate calling, or mission) and includes an analysis of the organization's external environment (which is a broader concept than the industry in which it is currently competing) and its key competencies (measured in terms of the customer benefits the organization is able to provide). It is a complex exercise which includes industry analysis, analysis of markets and competition, of customers and non-customers, and of key global trends that may not yet be apparent within the organization's immediate industry sector. But awareness is far more than an extensive data-gathering exercise. It is the ability to listen carefully and to put what you hear into some kind of context.

Awareness is the capacity to look at a situation as others would see it, to suspend emotional attachment for a moment, and look at the bigger picture. It is the hardest thing in the world to do and yet one of the most important. It does not mean that we buy in to the opinions and beliefs of other people, simply that we seek the space to view our lives from a position outside ourselves. This process is sometimes called a reality check, and it is as appropriate to organizations as it is to individuals.

A reality check is any tool, technique, method, or device that individuals or organizations use to provide feedback on their place in the world. Reality checks include tools and techniques that are recognised as strategic (such as industry analysis, competitor analysis, and so on) and many others that are not (customer research, employee feedback, or merely reading trade magazines). In fact *any* exercise to increase organizational awareness is an important part of the strategic process whether it normally has a strategic label or not.

The purpose of the reality check is to ensure that organizational strategy is based on an objective view of how the outside world really is, rather than on how the organization would like it to be. Unfortunately, knowledge of the real world is very often held in inverse proportion to levels of seniority. Those at the lower end of the organization (or at the customer interface) often have a much more accurate view of how the organization is performing than those who control the organization above them. For this reason, reality checks are not some centralized function (perhaps located in the finance area) but an on-going process that pervades the whole organization. Where this is not the case, organizational strategy often fails the most rudimentary common sense test. Common sense, as someone once wisely pointed out, is anything but common!

4. KNOW YOUR CUSTOMERS

Having a clear picture of the future, and being able to muster the energy to pursue that vision, are both vital to an organization if it is to survive.

However, corporate willpower and a sense of direction are not enough in themselves. No organizational future is complete or meaningful unless a company recognizes that it must take into account the people who truly hold the power of life or death over any company – its customers. Companies that get a down-turned thumb from their customers are on a rocky road indeed. UK retailers Marks & Spencer, for example, have learned this lesson the hard way.

There is no shortage of material on the importance of customers. Many writers stress the nature of customer relationships as long term partnerships in which the organization needs to delight its customers constantly by exceeding, rather than simply meeting, their expectations. Certainly, there is no substitute for talking directly with customers if an organization wants an objective view of how well it is succeeding at meeting their needs right now. Unfortunately, as we know from our personal lives, there is much more to maintaining a true partnership than talking; it takes work – and lots of it. True partnerships are complex, long-term relationships, which require honesty, trust, and a willingness to change, if they are to survive and prosper. Not surprisingly, it is in these areas that many organizations fall down.

As with economic and strategic analysis, there are a myriad tools and techniques to capture customer feedback, such as questionnaires, interviews, focus groups and other survey methodologies. These are useful, but they have a tendency to be framed unconsciously in such a way that customer feedback merely mirrors what the organization wants to hear. True customer orientation is much more than this; it requires an attitude of mind that integrates the customer into the organizational decision-making process. Simply put, it is a *way of life*.

This does not necessarily mean meeting all the wishes of customers. The most difficult thing for organizations is to know when:

» To lead the customer (taking the customer to a new place through new product or service opportunities),
» To contradict the customer (when it is genuinely in the customer's interest to do so), and
» Not to service a particular customer need (if it cannot be serviced profitably).

Ironically, organizations that continuously react to the *current* needs of the customer often fail to anticipate *future* needs.

One of the critical misunderstandings in customer research today is to mistake customer satisfaction for customer loyalty. Many organizations measure customer satisfaction regularly and assume that positive satisfaction ratings equate with a high degree of customer loyalty. Unfortunately, this is rarely the case. Research shows that this assumption is deeply flawed because the relationship between customer satisfaction and customer loyalty is not linear. In reality, customers need to be completely satisfied before they are willing to develop a committed relationship with an organization or its products and services.

5. EVALUATION AND SELECTION OF STRATEGIC OPTIONS

A number of factors have to be considered in selecting a preferred strategy. Each option has to be assessed for suitability in terms of resources, congruence in terms of overall strategic logic, and cultural fit within the organization. An organization will need to summarize the advantages and disadvantages of each strategic option, noting both internal constraints and external risk:

» Internal constraints include resources available, knowledge of new markets and products, and the cultural adaptability of the organization to new opportunities;
» External risks include possible reactions from competitors, threats to market demand from legislation or substitution etc.

Table 10.1 Evaluating strategic options.

Strategic options and substrategies	Advantages	Disadvantages	Risk/Feasibility	
			Internal constraints	External risks

Other factors to be considered include the investment needs of each option, the likely financial performance (including cash flow), the effect of key stakeholder expectations, and the relevance to other parts of the organization. The evaluation of strategic options is often performed using a table such as the one shown in Table 10.1.

The final step in the choice of strategy is the ranking of strategic options to determine the preferred strategy. Although often forgotten, a "do nothing" option should be included for comparison purposes. The feasibility of strategies can be ranked on a number of criteria, the most common of which are:

» The degree of change from the current strategy
» The leadership which is in place
» The resources and organization which is in place
» Cultural constraints
» The expectation of primary stakeholders (particularly in the public sector).

Often the ranking is done in tabular format, with a numerical rating given to each option (say, using a scale of 1–5) (Table 10.2).

6. CREATIVITY

The capacity to look at problems from a different orientation is fundamental to the success of organizations. Organizations which transform their industries often do so by changing the existing rules of the

Table 10.2 Ranking of strategic options.

Strategic options	Feasibility					Choice – order of preference	Main Factors Influencing Choice
	Change in Strategy	Leader-ship	Resources	Culture	Over-all		

game within the industry. With the pace of change increasing and competitive advantage increasingly short lived, the need to be able to transcend the mind-set of the existing players in an industry, literally to re-invent the industry, is becoming far more important as a guarantor of future success. Yet, for something that is so important, we understand remarkably little about the creative process.

Some writers argue that creativity is a gift or talent which the fortunate few are born with. Others argue that creativity lies within *all* of us, and that it is part of our true nature, but remains blocked-off in some way for many of us. No matter what we believe about the origins of the creative process, it is increasingly important for organizations to understand the importance of releasing it.

Like all of the critical success factors underlying the change process, it is not easily controlled in the traditional sense because it is complex, and sits uncomfortably with hierarchical structures and rigid functional barriers. As a result, many organizations have introduced more flexibility for their naturally creative employees in areas such as product innovation and development. But this, by itself, is not enough. Major benefits accrue to organizations only when the entire organizational perspective changes from encouraging a few creative individuals to come up with the next big idea, to building innovation into the organization's philosophies and processes as a way of life. This involves cross-stimulation throughout the organization by connecting ideas, people, and systems that were previously separate, and by allowing a diversity of approach and experimentation to problems.

Equally important, it necessitates supporting, coaching, and mentoring at every level of the organization employees who may believe that they are not in the least creative. Only when creativity is allowed to flourish at this individual level will organizations really see the difference.

7. LEADERSHIP

Leadership lies at the heart of successful change. The leader carries the torch for the organization, ignites the passion for change within it, and acts as a catalyst for that change. He or she is the ultimate custodian of the organizational vision. Leadership is sometimes referred to as the *temple of intentionality*, as it embodies the will to act within an organization. It is the element of leadership that is widely recognized when researchers ask groups to name great leaders. Groups often identify powerful political and military figures such as Winston Churchill, Alexander the Great, Ghengis Khan, Margaret Thatcher, Gandhi, Martin Luther King, Julius Caesar, Hitler (not all leaders are necessarily good), John F. Kennedy and others who epitomise this will to act in a way that inspires others to follow.

Yet there is another equally important aspect of leadership; one which focuses on maintaining relationships among group members. This is often not recognized at first, although groups sometimes identify spiritual figures such as Jesus, Buddha and Mother Theresa their list of great leaders. Nevertheless this aspect is fundamental to effective leadership, allowing the leader to sustain the people involved in the process of creating a *shared* vision for the organization. Often it is born of great humanity and empathy for fellow human beings. Harold Wilson, the former British Labour Prime Minister, wrote of Winston Churchill:

> "There was his great quality of humanity. The man who could move armies and navies and embrace the world in one strategic sweep could himself be moved to uncontrollable and unashamed tears at the sight of an old soul's cheerfulness in a shelter, or of a

street of devastated houses, at the thought of the human realities which lay behind the war communiqués.''

We do not fully understand leadership. Some writers argue that leaders truly create the future, others that they themselves are a product of the greater forces that shape humanity, albeit that they are far more attuned than others to the *zeitgeist*, the spirit of the times. Howard Gardner, a leading authority on leadership, argues that leaders are all those who,

> ''by word and/or personal example, markedly influence the behaviors, thoughts, and/or feelings of a significant number of their fellow human beings.''
> *"Leading Minds: An Anatomy of Leadership", Harper Collins,*
> *New York 1996*

Gardner emphasizes the ability of leaders to tell or embody stories that speak to other people and describes a continuum of leadership that starts with indirect leadership, exerted through written work or other symbolic communication, and progresses to direct leadership of the sort exercised by world leaders through speeches and other means.

There is a great deal more that could be said about leadership. For our purpose, however, we need only make one final observation. At the heart of leadership there lies a paradox, which was captured succinctly by Lao Tsu:

> ''The wicked leader is he whom people despise:
> The good leader is he whom people revere:
> The great leader is he of whom the people say, 'We did it ourselves.'''

8. TRUST

Trust needs to be earned. Common sense tells us that it is unwise to trust someone whom we do not know well. Moreover, trust is earned on the basis of actions not words; our ability to ''walk the talk,'' and the extent that we are committed to the same values and objectives as our colleagues. The peace activist Dorothy Day described it like this:

"True obedience is a matter of love, which makes it voluntary, not by fear or force." Creating an environment of trust and integrity within an organization is an incremental process that happens over time.

As human beings we have often spent a lifetime building sophisticated defensive mechanisms and barriers to protect ourselves and our individual integrity, and these are not easily dismantled. For many of us, our natural assumption is that our working environment is not safe and we behave accordingly. For good reasons, the actions of employees reflect the real beliefs, values, and norms that drive patterns of behavior within an organization ('the way things are *really* done around here') and not the formal and lofty pronouncements of aspiration.

Above all, trust is an intensely personal process; we trust individuals, not abstract concepts such as "the organization." This implies that trust is built within smaller groupings or teams within the organization, not by central directives from on high. It implies an unrelenting commitment to the truth at all levels of the organization. It also implies a willingness to bring to the surface cultural issues that may be unpalatable for the organization and to communicate these up, down and across the organization without fear of incrimination or ridicule. In short, to uncover the hidden dimension or shadow side of organizational culture. This demands great honesty, courage, and openness in any organization. It can also be a necessity of business survival as Gerard Egan, professor of psychology at Loyola University of Chicago, points out:

> "Managers are increasingly being forced into the role of managing chaos and change. While the technology of such change is comparatively straightforward and easy, the politics of change can prove impossible. Thus the best managers are always looking for ways to become more adept at dealing with the shadow side of the organization – the unspoken, unacknowledged, behind-the-scenes stuff that stands in the way of getting things done efficiently or even getting things done at all. In today's organizational and business climate, becoming skilled at behind-the-scenes management is not an amenity but a necessity. Failure to deal with the shadow side of change can lead to failure of the business itself."
>
> *"Working the Shadow Side: A Guide to Positive Behind-the-Scenes Management", Jossey-Bass, San Francisco 1994*

9. MAKE IT HAPPEN

There is a well-known four-letter acronym – JFDI – which, in the Parental Guidance version, stands for Just Flipping-well Do It. "Making it happen" is about the desire to get on and take action, and to do it to a high standard. For the company strategy, this is the point where the rubber hits the road.

Implementing strategy is normally about implementing change. Implementing change is often painful and it is always messy. In order to get to the future an organization needs to deal with both hard issues (such as re-engineering business processes, developing new technology, and implementing flexible production systems), and the many soft issues that result from human beings working closely together. Since the latter involves recognising and changing the culture of the organization, it is never straightforward. John Kotter, professor of Leadership at Harvard Business School, puts it succinctly:

> "In the final analysis, change sticks when it becomes the 'way we do things around here,' when it seeps into the bloodstream of the corporate body. Until new behaviors are rooted in social norms and shared values, they are subject to degradation as soon as the pressure for change is removed . . . In reality, even successful change efforts are messy and full of surprises."
> *"Why transformation efforts fail", Harvard Business Review*
> *March/April 1995*

The way in which the change process is managed is absolutely critical to its success. It demands absolute commitment from those at the top, good communication up, down, and across the organization, and significant levels of trust in people throughout the organization. But more than this it requires time. Making significant change is a long-term process. Increasingly, for many organizations it needs to become a way of life. This is not easy, a point nicely captured by the writer Dan Millman:

> "Everyone wants to change, but not everyone wants it enough to go through the period of initiation and discomfort. We may think we have the will to change, but we really only have the

whim to change ... Change doesn't happen until we commit to it (and) commitment means no matter what. When we commit to a relationship, we stop wondering whether someone out there might make an even better partner for us. If we commit to a career, we give it our best and waste no time toying with other possibilities. The feeling of commitment doesn't come naturally. We have to develop it, and earn it."

"No Ordinary Moments", HJ Kramer Inc., Novato, California
1992

10. MEASURE YOUR PERFORMANCE

The 1990s have witnessed dramatic changes in performance measurement resulting from the increasingly sophisticated use of IT, the failure of conventional management accounting techniques, and the integration of financial performance measures into the strategic management system as a whole. The most important innovation in this field is probably the development of the *balanced scorecard* (a strategic management system which supplements financial performance measures with customer, internal business process, and innovation and learning measures) which has been developed by Robert Kaplan and David Norton of the Harvard Business School. The balanced scorecard is designed to enable companies to track financial results while simultaneously monitoring progress in building the capabilities and acquiring the intangible assets they need for future growth.

Whichever tools or sets of measures are adopted, gaining feedback on performance is crucial. Without it, a company has no idea whether it should be maintaining the *status quo* or instituting radical change. Ignorance may be bliss, but information is the stuff of improvement.

The best evaluation systems have two important characteristics: balance and self-correction. They include a range of key performance indicators that provide the organization with a comprehensive view of current competitiveness and some advance warning of future position and prospects. These key performance indicators are integrated into a strategic management system, such as the balanced scorecard, which clearly emphasises performance evaluation as a key part of the strategic process. Managers also need to consider the process of evaluation. A system of remote management control tends to lead to information being shuffled up and down the organizational hierarchy, risking delay and distortion at each stage. By pushing the awareness of key performance indicators down into the organization, employees can develop a range of supplementary measures to help them evaluate their own day-to-day performance against the broader strategic vision of the organization.

The best evaluation systems are part of the fabric of the organization; a way of life with checks and balances to ensure that the information coming into the organization is appropriate and balanced. They are not simply controlling mechanisms to ensure that top-down targets are reached. Instead, short-term targets and action plans are tightly linked to the organization's shared vision which continually evolves to take account of new information from external markets, competition and the macro-economic environment. Above all, evaluation is not something that is done to people. It is a way in which people choose to identify objectively how the business is doing, break down long-term strategy into a series of achievable short-term goals and action plans, and monitor progress towards a mutually-defined sense of the future.

That said, the best way to treat most financial information is with a healthy degree of scepticism; it is an essential part of the decision-making process but it should not become the tail that wags the dog. There may be very good reasons for some activities to make a loss (launching a new business venture, or the costs attached to recovering a valued customer), but we should be aware that this loss is occurring. Attention to the bottom line is, on the whole, a good thing as long as it does not become a pre-occupation at the expense of the long-term development of the business.

Frequently Asked Questions (FAQs)

Q1: What is strategy?

A: Strategy is about developing an understanding of the present situation (Where are we now?), the desired future position (Where do we want to be?) and the path to take the organization from its present position into the future (How do we get there?). See Chapter 2.

Q2: What are the origins of strategy?

A: Business strategy derived much of its early shape from military models of planning and implementation. See Chapter 3.

Q3: Given that the world is becoming more and more unpredictable, is strategy still relevant?

A: Yes, these days, strategy does not presume that the future is entirely "knowable"; rather it provides frameworks and tools for managing the "unknowable". See Chapter 3.

Q4: Who are the key figures in strategy over the past 20 years or so?

A: From the publication of his book *Competitive Strategy* in 1980 to a Harvard Business Review article on "Strategy and the Internet", published in March 2001, Michael Porter has been the single most influential figure. See Chapters 3 and 8.

Q5: Is there a dominant school of strategy?

A: Not any more. There was a commonly held view that strategy was a rational planning process that could be applied in an essentially predictable world but the world has changed over the past 15 to 20 years. Now there are any number of perspectives. See Chapter 6.

Q6: What impact does globalization have on strategic thinking?

A: There are several implications for anybody involved in formulating or implementing strategy in a business, no matter what its size, location or industry sector. See Chapter 5.

Q7: And what about the impact of new technology?

A: The new economy has had a significant effect on strategic thinking in many business sectors. Despite the current difficulties faced by the dot-com world, some e-models will undoubtedly survive. See Chapter 4.

Q8: How valuable are case studies on strategy?

A: Case studies very rarely produce solutions that can be transplanted wholesale into a different company. Nevertheless, they will always throw up relevant questions and may often suggest a way forward. See Chapter 7.

Q9: So where is strategy heading in the future?

A: Strategy is always on the lookout for appropriate tools and lenses for improving future competitiveness. It seems likely that the science of complexity will provide some useful perspectives over the coming years. See Chapter 6.

Q10: How can I find out more?

A: There is no problem getting hold of information about strategy – there are literally thousands of books and articles published every year. The trick is to distinguish the useful from the irrelevant or derivative. See Chapter 9.

About the Authors

JOHN MIDDLETON

John Middleton is the founder of the Bristol Management Research Centre. Recognized as a leading expert in personal and systems thinking technologies, he works as a coach and consultant with individuals and organizations who are determined to make best use of the future.

From 1996 to 2001 he published and edited *Future Filter*, a bi-monthly business digest for the new economy.

He has written two books – *Smart Things to Know about your Career* (Capstone, 2001) and *Writing the New Economy* (Capstone, 2000). His next book will be *The Ultimate Strategy Library*, due to be published in 2002.

His e-mail address is: john@hotpotatoes.co.uk

BOB GORZYNSKI

Bob Gorzynski has worked extensively in the fields of strategy, change management and customer care with both large international organizations and at owner-manager level. After spending 10 years in corporate finance and strategy in blue chip companies, he has specialized in aligning the technical and the human aspects of strategic change. He currently specializes in the media, entertainment and retail sectors.

Index

Richard Pascale - Managing on the Edge
Surfing on the Edge of Chaos

Johnson + Scholes - Exploring Corporate Strategy

Hamel + Prahalad - Competing for the Future